THE *Lyric* LIBRARY

Broadway
Volume II

Complete Lyrics for 200 Songs
From 116 Musicals

HAL•LEONARD®

Other books in *The Lyric Library*:

Broadway Volume I

Christmas

Classic Rock

Contemporary Christian

Country

Early Rock 'n' Roll

Love Songs

Pop/Rock Ballads

ISBN 0-634-04521-0

Library of Congress cataloguing-in-publication data has been applied for.

Visit Hal Leonard Online at
www.halleonard.com

Preface

What would the history of popular song be without the Broadway musical? And what would the Broadway musical be without the master lyric writers who found the seemingly inevitable words that sit on the notes of timeless tunes? The list goes on and on of great stage lyricists who defined the sensibilites of their times: Irving Berlin, the team of Betty Comden and Adolph Green, Fred Ebb, Ira Gershwin, Oscar Hammerstein, Lorenz Hart, Jerry Herman, Alan Jay Lerner, Frank Loesser, Cole Porter, Tim Rice, Stephen Sondheim…

Lyrics in the British influenced operetta era on Broadway before the 1920s tended to be artificial, purplish and high-flown. In contrast, the lyrics of Lorenz Hart and Cole Porter, among others, took American vernacular speech and turned it into comfortable, casual verse. The best standards from musicals written between the two world wars remain fresh even today, not only due to unforgettable melodies, but also because the lyrics cleverly capture and condense everyday, on-the-street American language.

Most of the mature book musicals of the 1940s, 1950s and 1960s, by Rodgers & Hammerstein, Lerner & Loewe, Frank Loesser, Jerry Herman and other major figures, produced songs that were more specific to character and plot. That didn't prevent many of them from becoming famous as stand-alone songs: the idealized longing for romance of "Some Enchanted Evening" from *South Pacific*, the rousing anthem "There's No Business Like Show Business" from *Annie Get Your Gun*, the gentle lyricism of "On the Street Where You Live" from *My Fair Lady*, and the torch song regret of "If He Walked into My Life" from *Mame*, among dozens of others.

A modern, urban point of view emerged in Broadway lyrics of the 1960s and 1970s, especially from top talents such as Fred Ebb and Stephen Sondheim. A few years later, grand romanticism came to the stage in the mega-hits *The Phantom of the Opera* and *Les Misérables*, with sweeping lyrics in broad, expressive strokes.

New writers continue to find fresh turns of phrase to mirror contemporary thought as the musical moves ahead in a new century. And the success of professional revivals proves that a well-crafted, inspired and classic show has timeless appeal.

The houselights still dim all over the world every night as the first notes of a musical are heard. The dawn of every new experience in the theatre for a lover of musicals forever has the promise of Lerner's line from "Camelot:"

"In short, there's simply not a more congenial spot for happ'ly-ever-aftering…"

Contents

Broadway
Volume II

Ace in the Hole

Words and Music by Cole Porter

from *Let's Face It*

If my brain is simply uncanny
When I'm in a spot,
When I'm in a spot, it's true,
I always know what to do,
It's because my clever old granny
Knew oh, such a lot,
She was older than God,
So it doesn't seem odd
If granny knew oh, such a lot.

To steady me,
And ready me,
For the battle of men and mice,
Each night, gran'mummy
Would pat on my tummy
And give me this good advice,
This perfect advice!

Sad times
May follow your tracks,
Bad times
May bar you from Saks,
Add times
When Satan in slacks
Breaks down your self-control.

Maybe,
As often it goes,
Your Abie
May tire of his Rose,
So Baby,
This rule I propose,
Always have an ace in the hole.

Ain't Misbehavin'

Words by Andy Razaf
Music by Thomas "Fats" Waller and Harry Brooks

from *Ain't Misbehavin'*

Verse:
Boy:
Tho's it's a fickle age
With flirting all the rage,
Here is one bird with self-control;
Happy inside my cage.
I know who I love best,
Thumbs down for all the rest,
My love was given, heart and soul,
So it can withstand the test.

Refrain:
No one to talk with,
All by myself.
No one to walk with,
But I'm happy on the shelf.
Ain't misbehavin',
I'm savin' my love for you.

I know for certain,
The one I love.
I'm through with flirtin',
It's just you I'm thinkin' of.
Ain't misbehavin',
I'm savin' my love for you.

Like Jack Horner,
In the corner,
Don't go nowhere.
What do I care?
Your kisses are worth waitin' for;
Believe me.

I don't stay out late,
Don't care to go.
I'm home about eight,
Just me and my radio.
Ain't misbehavin',
I'm saving my love for you.

Verse:
Girl:
Your type of man is rare,
I know you really care.
That's why my conscience never sleeps,
When you're away somewhere.
Sure was a lucky day,
When fate sent you my way,
And made you mine alone for keeps,
Ditto to all you say.

Repeat Refrain

All Good Gifts

Words and Music by Stephen Schwartz

from the Musical *Godspell*

We plow the fields and scatter
The good seed on the land,
But it is fed and watered
By God's almighty hand.

He sends the snow in winter,
The warmth to swell the grain,
The breezes and the sunshine,
And soft refreshing rain.

Refrain:
All good gifts around us
Are sent from heaven above.
Then thank the Lord,
O thank the Lord for all His love.

We thank Thee, then O Father,
For all things bright and good,
The seed time and the harvest,
Our life, our health, our food.

No gifts have we to offer,
For all Thy love imparts,
But that which Thou desirest,
Our humble, thankful hearts.

Refrain

I really want to thank You, Lord,
I want to thank You, Lord,
Thank You for all of Your love,
I want to thank You, Lord,
I want to thank You for love.
Oh, thank You, Lord!

All I Need Is the Girl

Words by Stephen Sondheim
Music by Jule Styne

from *Gypsy*

Once my clothes were shabby.
Tailors called me "cabbie."
So I took a vow,
Said, "This bum'll be beau Brummell."

Now I'm smooth and snappy,
Now my tailor's happy.
I'm the cat's meow!
My wardrobe is a wow!

Paris silk,
Harris tweed,
There's only one thing I need.

Got my tweed pressed,
Got my best vest,
All I need now is the girl!
Got my striped tie,
Got my hopes high,
Got the time and the place
And I got rhythm,
Now all I need's the girl to go with 'em.

If she'll just appear,
We'll take this big town for a whirl.
And if she'll say,
"My darling, I'm yours,"
I'll throw away my striped tie
And my best pressed tweed,
All I really need is the girl!

All I've Got to Get Now Is My Man

Words and Music by Cole Porter

from *Panama Hattie*

If I'm in a high state of jitter,
If I typify glow and glitter,
If you wonder why
I'm touring heaven with the swallows,
Then hark ye,
And mark ye,
What follows.

Got the gown,
Got the veil,
Got the ring,
It's a whale,
Got the crowd in the church,
Got the minister on his perch,
All I've got to get now is my man.

Picked the house,
Not too far,
Open fire,
Open bar,
Second floor, what a treat,
Such a beautiful bridal suite,
All I've got to get now is my man.

Yes, all I've got to get now is my man.
Yes, all I've got to get now is my man.
'Cause ev'rything is set now,
I've got a complete layette now,
And all I've got to get now is my man.

Ev'rything's set now,
Got the layette now,
All I got to get now is my man.

All of You

Words and Music by Cole Porter

from *Silk Stockings*

I love the looks of you, the lure of you.
The sweet of you, the pure of you.
The eyes, the arms, the mouth of you.
The east, west, north and the south of you.
I'd love to gain complete control of you.
And handle even the heart and soul of you.
So love, at least, a small percent of me, do.
For I love all of you.

Alternate Verse:
I love the looks of you, the lure of you.
I'd love to make a tour of you.
The eyes, the arms, the mouth of you.
The east, west, north, and the south of you.
I'd love to gain complete control of you.
And handle even the heart and soul of you.
So love, at least, a small percent of me, do.
For I love all of you.

Alone at the Drive-In Movie

Lyric and Music by Warren Casey and Jim Jacobs

from *Grease*

I'm all alone,
At the drive-in movie,
It's a feeling
That ain't too groovy,
Watching werewolves without you.

Gee, it's no fun
Drinking beer in the back seat,
All alone
Just ain't too neat,
At the passion pit, wanting you.

And when the intermission elf
Moves the clock's hands,
While he's eating ev'rything
Sold at the stand.

When there's one minute to go,
'Til the lights go down low,
I'll be holding the speaker knobs,
Missing you so.

Can't believe it,
Unsteamed windows I can see through,
Might as well be in an igloo,
'Cause the heater doesn't work
As good as you.
(Baby, come back.)

Another Op'nin', Another Show

Words and Music by Cole Porter

from *Kiss Me, Kate*

Another op'nin', another show,
In Philly, Boston, or Baltimo'e.
A chance for stage folks to say, "hello,"
Another op'nin' of another show.

Another job that you hope, at last,
Will make your future forget your past.
Another pain, where the ulcers grow,
Another op'nin' of another show!

Four weeks you rehearse and rehearse.
Three weeks and it couldn't be worse.
One week, will it ever be right?
Then out of the hat it's that big first night!

The overture is about to start.
You cross your fingers and hold your heart.
It's curtain time and away we go.
Another op'nin' of another show.

Anyone Can Whistle

Words and Music by Stephen Sondheim

from *Anyone Can Whistle*

Anyone can whistle,
That's what they say,
Easy.
Anyone can whistle,
Any old day,
Easy.
It's all so simple:
Relax, let go, let fly!
So someone tell me why can't I?

I can dance a tango,
I can read Greek,
Easy.
I can slay a dragon
Any old week,
Easy!
What's hard is simple,
What's natural comes hard.
Maybe you could show me
How to let go,
Lower my guard,
Learn to be free.
Maybe if you can whistle,
Whistle for me.

As If We Never Said Goodbye

Music by Andrew Lloyd Webber
Lyrics by Don Black and Christopher Hampton,
with contributions by Amy Powers

from *Sunset Boulevard*

I don't know why I'm frightened,
I know my way around here.
The cardboard trees, the painted seas,
    the sound here.
Yes, a world to rediscover,
But I'm not in any hurry,
And I need a moment.

The whispered conversations in
    overcrowded hallways,
The atmosphere as thrilling here
As always.
Feel the early morning madness,
Feel the magic in the making.
Why, everything's as if we never
    said goodbye.

I've spent so many mornings,
Just trying to resist you.
I'm trembling now, you can't know how
    I've missed you,
Missed the fairytale adventures
In this ever-spinning playground.
We were young together.

I'm coming out of makeup,
The light's already burning.
Not long until the cameras will
    start turning,
And the early morning madness,
And the magic in the making,
Yes, everything's as if we never
    said goodbye.

I don't want to be alone,
That's all in the past.
This world's waited long enough,
I've come home at last,

And this time will be bigger,
And brighter than we knew it.
So watch me fly, we all know I can do it.
Could I stop my hand from shaking?
Has there ever been a moment
With so much to live for?

The whispered conversations in
    overcrowded hallways,
So much to say, not just today, but always.
We'll have early morning madness,
We'll have magic in the making.
Yes, everything's as if we never said goodbye,
Yes, everything's as if we never said goodbye.
We taught the world new ways to dream.

Be Kind to Your Parents

Words and Music by Harold Rome

from *Fanny*

Here's a piece of good advice.
Think it over once or twice.

Refrain:
Be kind to your parents,
Though they don't deserve it.
Remember they're grown-ups,
A difficult stage of life.

They're apt to be nervous,
And overexcited,
Confused from their daily
Storm and strife.

Just keep in mind,
Though it sounds odd, I know,
Most parents once were children
Long ago. Incredible!

So treat them with patience
And sweet understanding,
In spite of the foolish things they do.
Some day you may wake up,
And find you're a parent too!

Refrain

Beauty School Dropout

Lyric and Music by Warren Casey and Jim Jacobs

from *Grease*

Your story's sad to tell,
A teenage ne'er-do-well,
Most mixed up non-delinquent on the block.
Your future's so unclear now,
What's left of your career now?
Can't even get a trade-in on your smock.

Beauty school dropout,
No graduation day for you,
Beauty school dropout,
Missed your mid-terms and
    flunked shampoo,
Well, at least you could have taken time
To wash and clean your clothes up,
After spending all that dough
To have the doctor fix your nose up.

Baby, get movin',
Why keep your feeble hopes alive?
What are ya provin'?
You got the dream but not the drive.
If you go for your diploma,
You could join a steno-pool,
Turn in your teasing comb
And go back to high school.

Beauty school dropout,
Hangin' around the corner store,
Beauty school dropout,
It's about time you knew the score,
Well, they couldn't teach you anything,
You think you're such a looker,
But no customer would go to you,
Unless she was a hooker.

Baby, don't sweat it,
You're not cut out to hold a job,
Better forget it,
Who wants their hair done by a slob?
Now, your bangs are curled,
Your lashes twirled,
But still the world is cruel.
Wipe off that angel face
And go back to high school.

ADDITIONAL LYRICS
Baby, you blew it!
You put our good advice to shame.
How could you do it?
Betcha Dear Abby'd say the same.
Guess there's no way to get through to you,
No matter who may try.
Might as well go back
To that malt shop in the sky.
Yah.

Before I Gaze at You Again

Words by Alan Jay Lerner
Music by Frederick Loewe

from *Camelot*

Before I gaze at you again,
I'll need a time for tears.
Before I gaze at you again,
Let hours turn to years.
I have so much forgetting to do,
Before I try to gaze again at you.

Stay away until you cross my mind
Barely once a day;
Till the moment I awake and find
I can smile and say:

That I can gaze at you again,
Without a blush or qualm,
My eyes a-shine like new again,
My manner poised and calm.
Stay far away,
My love, far away.
Till I forget I gazed at you today.
Today, today.

The Best of Times

Music and Lyric by Jerry Herman

from *La Cage Aux Folles*

Refrain 1:
The best of times is now.
What's left of summer but a faded rose?
The best of times is now.
As for tomorrow, well, who knows?
Who knows?
Who knows?

Refrain 2:
So hold this moment fast
And live and love as hard as you know how.
And make this moment last,
Because the best of times is now,
Is now,
Is now.

Now,
Not some forgotten yesterday.
Now,
Tomorrow is too far away.

Refrain 2

Refrain 1

Refrain 2

The Best Things in Life Are Free

Music and Lyrics by B.G. DeSylva, Lew Brown and Ray Henderson

from *Good News!*

The moon belongs to ev'ryone,
The best things in life are free,
The stars belong to ev'ryone,
They gleam there for you and me.

The flowers in Spring,
The robins that sing,
The sunbeams that shine,
They're yours, they're mine!

And love can come to ev'ryone,
The best things in life are free.

Blue Skies

Words and Music by Irving Berlin

from *Betsy*

I was blue, just as blue as I could be.
Every day was a cloudy day for me.
Then good luck came a-knocking at my door.
Skies were gray but they're not gray anymore.

Blue skies,
Smiling at me.
Nothing but blue skies
Do I see.

Blue birds,
Singing a song
Nothing but bluebirds
All day long,

Never saw the sun shining so bright.
Never saw things going so right.
Noticing the days hurrying by
When you're in love, my how they fly.

Blue days,
All of them gone.
Nothing but blue skies
From now on.

Bring Him Home

Music by Claude-Michel Schönberg
Lyrics by Herbert Kretzmer and Alain Boublil

from *Les Misérables*

God on high,
Hear my prayer.
In my need,
You have always been there.

He is young,
He's afraid.
Let him rest,
Heaven blessed.

Bring him home,
Bring him home,
Bring him home.
He's like the son
I might have known.
If God had granted me a son.
The summers die,
One by one.
How soon they fly,
On and on.
And I am old,
And will be gone.

Bring him peace,
Bring him joy.
He is young,
He is only a boy.

You can take,
You can give,
Let him be,
Let him live.

If I die,
Let me die,
Let him live.
Bring him home.

A Bushel and a Peck

By Frank Loesser

from *Guys and Dolls*

I love you a bushel and a peck,
A bushel and a peck and a hug around the neck,
Hug around the neck and a barrel and a heap,
Barrel and a heap and I'm talkin' in my sleep
About you,
About you.

Refrain:
'Cause I love you a bushel and a peck,
Y'bet your purty neck I do.
Doodle oodle oodle,
Doodle oodle oodle,
A-doodle oodle oodle ooo.

I love you a bushel and a peck,
A bushel and a peck, tho' you make my heart a wreck,
Make my heart a wreck and you make my life a mess,
Make my life a mess, yes a mess of happiness,
About you,
About you.

Refrain

I love you a bushel and a peck,
A bushel and a peck and it beats me all to heck,
Beats me all to heck how I'll ever tend the farm,
Ever tend the farm when I wanna keep my arm
About you,
About you.

Refrain

Brotherhood of Man

By Frank Loesser

from *How to Succeed in Business Without Really Trying*

Finch:
Now, you may join the Elks, my friend,
And I may join the Shriners.
And other men may carry cards
As members of the Diners.
Still others wear a golden key,
Or small Greek letter pin.
But I have learned there's one great club
That all of us are in.

There is a brotherhood of man,
A benevolent brotherhood of man,
A noble tie that binds
All human hearts and minds
Into one brotherhood of man.

Refrain 1:
Your lifelong membership is free.
Keep a-giving each brother all you can.
Oh, aren't you proud to be
In that fraternity,
The great, big brotherhood of man?

One man may seem incompetent,
Another not make sense,
While others look like quite a waste
Of company expense.
They need a brother's leadership,
So please don't do them in,
Remember mediocrity
Is not a mortal sin.

Finch and Men:
They're [We're] in the brotherhood of man,
Dedicated to giving all we can.
Finch:
Oh, aren't you proud to be
In that fraternity,
Men:
The great, big brotherhood of man?

Womper (Spoken):
No kidding!

Womper (Sung):
Is there really a brotherhood of man?
On the level,
A brotherhood of man?

Biggley and Men:
Yes, you're a brother,
You are a brother!
Oh yes, oh yes.
A noble tie that binds
All human hearts and minds,

Womper:
Into one brotherhood of man.
Men:
Oh, yes.

Men:
Refrain 1

Miss Jones:
You, you got me,
Me, I got you-oo,
You-oo.

Miss Jones:
Refrain 2:
Oh, that noble feeling,
Feels like bells are pealing,
Down with double dealing,
Oh, brother.
You, you got me,
Me, I got you-oo.
You-oo.

Miss Jones and Men:
Refrain 2

Men:
Oh, that noble feeling,
(Oh!)
Feels like bells are pealing,
Down with double dealing,

Miss Jones and Men:
Oh, brother.
You, you got me,
Me, I got you-oo.
You-oo.

All:
Refrain 1

Buddy's Blues

Words and Music by Stephen Sondheim

from *Follies*

Hello, folks, we're into the Follies!
First, though, folks,
   we'll pause for a mo'.
No, no, folks, you'll still get your jollies,
It's just I got a problem that I think you
   should know.

See, I've been very perturbed of late,
   very upset,
Very betwixt and between.
The things that I want
   I don't seem to get.
The things that I get…
You know what I mean?

I've got those
"God, why don't you love me,
Oh you do, I'll see you later"
Blues,
That "Long as you ignore me,
You're the only thing that matters"
Feeling.

Refrain:
That "If I'm good enough for you,
You're not good enough,"
And "Thank you for the present,
But what's wrong with it?" stuff.

Those "Don't come any closer
'Cause you know how much I love you"
Feelings,
Those "Tell me that you love me,
Oh you did, I gotta run now"
Blues.

Spoken:
Margie?
Sung:
She says she really loves me,
(I love you.)
She says.
She says she really cares.
(I care. I care.)
She says that I'm her hero,
(My hero.)
She says.
I'm perfect, she swears.
(You're perfect, goddamn it.)
She says that if we parted,
(If we parted—)
She says,
She says that she'd be sick.
(Bleah.)
She says she's mine forever,
(Forever.)
She says.
I gotta get outta here quick!

I've got those
"Whisper how I'm better than I think,
But what do you know?"
Blues.
That "Why do you keep telling me I stink,
When I adore you?"
Feeling.

That "Say I'm all the world to you,
You're out of your mind,"
"I know there's someone else
And I could kiss your behind,"

Those "You say I'm terrific
But your taste was always rotten"
Feelings,
Those "Go away, I need you,"
"Come to me, I'll kill you,"
"Darling, I'll do anything
To keep you with me till you
Tell me that you love me,
Oh you did, now beat it, will you?"
Blues.

Spoken:
Sally. Oh, Sally.
Sung:
She says she loves another,
(Another.)
She says,
A fella she prefers.
(Furs. Furs.)
She says that he's her idol.
(Idol idol idol idol.)
She says.
"Ideal," she avers.
(You deal. Avers?!)

She says that anybody
(Buddy, Bleah!)
Would suit her more than I.
(Aye, aye, aye.)
She says that I'm a washout,
(A washout!)
She says.
I love her so much I could die!

I've got those
"God, why don't you love me,
Oh you do, I'll see you later"
Blues,
(Bla bla blues,)
That "Long as you ignore me,
You're the only thing that matters"
Feeling.
(Feeling.)

Refrain

Those "Don't come any closer
Cause you know how much I love you"
Feelings,
Those "If you will, then I can't,"
"If you don't, then I gotta,"
"Give it to me, I don't want it,"
"If you won't I gotta have it,"
High, low,
Wrong, right,
Yes, no,
Black, white,
"God, why don't you love me,
Oh you do, I'll see you later"
Blues!

Button Up Your Overcoat

Words and Music by B.G. DeSylva, Lew Brown and Ray Henderson

from *Follow Thru*

Refrain:
Button up your overcoat,
When the wind is free,
Take good care of yourself,
You belong to me!

Eat an apple ev'ry day,
Get to bed by three,
Take good care of yourself,
You belong to me!

Be careful crossing streets,
Oo-oo!
Don't eat meats,
Oo-oo!
Cut out sweets,
Oo-oo!
You'll get a pain
And ruin your tum-tum!

Keep away from bootleg hootch,
When you're on a spree,
Take good care of yourself,
You belong to me!

Refrain

Wear your flannel underwear,
When you climb a tree,
Take good care of yourself,
You belong to me!

Don't sit on hornets' tails,
Oo-oo!
Or on nails,
Oo-oo!
Or third rails,
Oo-oo!
You'll get a pain
And ruin your tum-tum!

Don't go out with college boys,
When you're on a spree,
Take good care of yourself,
You belong to me.

Camelot

Words by Alan Jay Lerner
Music by Frederick Loewe

from *Camelot*

A law was made a distant moon ago here,
July and August cannot be too hot.
And there's a legal limit to the snow here,
In Camelot.

The winter is forbidden till December,
And exits March the second on the dot.
By order summer lingers
   through September,
In Camelot.

Camelot! Camelot!
I know it sounds a bit bizarre,
But in Camelot, Camelot,
That's how conditions are.

The rain may never fall till after sundown.
By eight the morning fog must disappear.
In short, there's simply not
A more congenial spot,
For happily-ever-aftering
Than here in Camelot!

The winter is forbidden till December,
And exits March the second on the dot.
By order summer lingers
   through September,
In Camelot.

Camelot! Camelot!
I know it gives a person pause,
But in Camelot, Camelot,
Those are the legal laws.

The snow may never slush upon the hillside.
By nine P.M. the moonlight must appear.
In short, there's simply not
A more congenial spot
For happily-ever-aftering
Than here in Camelot.

C'est Moi

Words by Alan Jay Lerner
Music by Frederick Loewe

from *Camelot*

Camelot!
Camelot!
In far off France I heard your call.
Camelot!
Camelot!
And here I am to give my all.
I know in my soul what you expect of me,
And all that and more I shall be!

A knight of the table round
    should be invincible.
Succeed where a less fantastic
    man would fail.
Climb a wall no one else can climb,
Cleave a dragon in record time,
Swim a moat in a coat of heavy iron mail.

No matter the pain he ought to be
    unwincable,
Impossible deeds should be his daily fare.
But where in the world
Is there in the world
A man so extraordinaire?

C'est moi! C'est moi!
I'm forced to admit!
'Tis I, I humbly reply.
That mortal who
These marvels can do,
C'est moi, c'est moi, 'tis I!

I've never lost in battle or game.
I'm simply the best by far.
When swords are cross'd,
'Tis always the same,
One blow and au revoir!

C'est moi! C'est moi!
So admir'bly fit,
A French Prometheus unbound.
And here I stand with valor untold,
Exception'lly brave, amazingly bold,
To serve at the Table Round!

The soul of a knight should be a thing
    remarkable,
His heart and his mind as pure as
    morning dew.
With a will and a self-restraint
That's the envy of ev'ry saint,
He could easily work a miracle or two!

To love and desire he ought to be
    unsparkable.
The ways of the flesh should offer no allure.
But where in the world
Is there in the world
A man so untouch'd and pure?
(Spoken:) C'est moi.

C'est moi! C'est moi,
I blush to disclose,
I'm far too noble to lie.
That man in whom
These qualities bloom,
C'est moi, c'est moi, 'tis I!

I've never stray'd from all I believe.
I'm bless'd with an iron will.
Had I been made
The partner of Eve,
We'd be in Eden still.

C'est moi! C'est moi,
The angels have chose
To fight their battles below.
And here I stand as pure as a pray'r,
Incredibly clean, with virtue to spare,
The godliest man I know!
(Spoken:) C'est moi!

Caravan

Words and Music by Duke Ellington, Irving Mills and Juan Tizol

from *Sophisticated Ladies*

Night and stars above that shine so bright,
The mystery of their fading light,
That shines upon our caravan.

Sleep upon my shoulder as we creep
Across the sands so I may keep,
This memory of our caravan.

This is so exciting
You are so inviting
Resting in my arms
As I thrill to the magic charms of you,

Beside me here beneath the blue
My dream of love is coming true
Within our desert caravan.

Close as Pages in a Book

Words by Dorothy Fields
Music by Sigmund Romberg

from *Up in Central Park*

We'll be close as pages in a book, my love and I.
So close we can share a single look, share every sigh.
So close that before I hear your laugh, my laugh breaks through;
And when a tear starts to appear,
My eyes grow misty too.

Our dreams won't come tumbling to the ground.
We'll hold them fast.
Darling, as the strongest book is bound,
We're bound to last.
Your life is my life and while life beats away in my heart,
We'll be as close as pages in a book.

Close Every Door

Music by Andrew Lloyd Webber
Lyrics by Tim Rice

from *Joseph and the Amazing Technicolor® Dreamcoat*

Close ev'ry door to me,
Hide all the world from me,
Bar all the windows
And shut out the light.

Do what you want with me,
Hate me and laugh at me,
Darken my daytime
And torture my night.

Refrain:
If my life were important,
I would ask, will I live or die,
But I know the answers lie
Far from this world.

Close ev'ry door to me,
Keep those I love from me,
Children of Israel
Are never alone.

For I know I shall find
My own peace of mind,
For I have been promised
A land of my own.

Just give me a number
Instead of my name,
Forget all about me,
And let me decay.

I do not matter,
I'm only one person,
Destroy me completely,
Then throw me away.

Refrain

For we know we shall find
Our own peace of mind,
For we have been promised
A land of our own.

Consider Yourself

Words and Music by Lionel Bart

from the Broadway Musical *Oliver!*

Consider yourself at home.
Consider yourself one of the family.
We've taken to you so strong,
It's clear we're going to get along.

Consider yourself well in.
Consider yourself part of the furniture.
There isn't a lot to spare.
Who cares, whatever we've got, we share.

If it should chance to be we should
    see some harder days,
Empty larder days, why grouse?
Always a chance to meet somebody to
    foot the bill,
Then drinks are on the house.

Consider yourself our mate.
We don't want to have no fuss.
For after some consideration we can state,
Consider yourself one of us.

Consider yourself at home.
Consider yourself one of the family.
We've taken to you so strong,
It's clear we're going to get along.

Consider yourself well in.
Consider yourself part of the furniture.
There isn't a lot to spare.
Who cares, whatever we've got, we share.

Nobody tries to be lah-di-dah and uppity.
There's a cup of tea for all.
Only it's wise to be handy wiv' a rolling pin
When the landlord comes to call!

Consider yourself our mate.
We don't want to have no fuss.
For after some consideration we can state,
Consider yourself one of us.

Could I Leave You

Words and Music by Stephen Sondheim

from *Follies*

Leave you? Leave you?
How could I leave you?
How could I go it alone?
Could I wave the years away,
With a quick good-bye?
How do you wipe tears away,
When your eyes are dry?

Sweetheart, lover,
Could I recover,
Give up the joys I have known?
Not to fetch your pills again,
Ev'ry day at five,
Not to give those dinners for ten
Elderly men from the U.N.,
How could I survive?

Could I leave you,
And your shelves of the World's Best Books,
And the evenings of martyred looks,
Cryptic sighs,
Sullen glares from those injured eyes?
Leave the quips with a sting,
Jokes with a sneer,
Passionless lovemaking, once a year?
Leave the lies,
Ill concealed,
And the wounds never healed
And the games not worth winning,
And—wait! I'm just beginning!

What, leave you? Leave you?
How could I leave you?
What would I do on my own?
Putting thoughts of you aside,
In the south of France,
Would I think of suicide?
Darling, shall we dance?

Could I live through the pain
On a terrace in Spain?
Would it pass?
It would pass.
Could I bury my rage
With a boy half your age,
In the grass?
Bet your ass.
But I've done that already.
Or didn't you know, love?
Tell me, how could I leave,
When I left long ago, love?

Could I leave you?
No, the point is,
Could you leave me?
Well, I guess you could
Leave me the house,
Leave me the flat,
Leave me the Braques and Chagalls
And all that.
You could leave me the stocks,
For sentiment's sake,
And ninety percent
Of the money you make,
And the rugs,
And the cooks,
Darling you keep the drugs,
Angel, you keep the books,
Honey, I'll take the grand,
Sugar, you keep the spinet
And all of our friends and…
Just wait a goddamn minute!

Oh, leave you? Leave you?
How could I leave you?
Sweetheart, I have to confess.
Could I leave you?
Yes.
Will I leave you?
Will I leave you?
(Spoken:) Guess!

Dancing on the Ceiling

Words by Lorenz Hart
Music by Richard Rodgers

dropped from *Simple Simon*
subsequently introduced in *Ever Green*

The world is lyrical
Because a miracle
Has brought my lover to me!
Though he's some other place,
His face I see.
At night I creep in bed,
And never sleep in bed,
But look above in the air.
And to my greatest joy,
My boy is there!
It is my prince who walks
Into my dreams and talks.

He dances overhead
On the ceiling, near my bed,
In my sight,
Through the night.

I try to hide in vain,
Underneath my counterpane,
There's my love,
Up above!

I whisper, "Go away, my lover,
It's not fair,"
But I'm so grateful to discover
He's still there.
I love my ceiling more
Since it is a dancing floor,
Just for my love.

Do-Re-Mi

Lyrics by Oscar Hammerstein II
Music by Richard Rodgers

from *The Sound of Music*

Let's start at the very beginning,
A very good place to start.
When you read you begin with—
A, B, C.
When you sing you begin with do re mi.

Do re mi?
Do re mi.
The first three notes just happen to be
Do Re Mi.
Doe—a deer, a female deer,
Ray—a drop of golden sun,
Me—a name I call myself,
Far—a long, long way to run,
Sew—a needle pulling thread,
La—a note to follow sew,
Tea—a drink with jam and bread.
That will bring us back to do!

Do re mi fa so la ti do.

Do You Hear the People Sing?

Music by Claude-Michel Schönberg
Lyrics by Herbert Kretzmer
Original Text by Alain Boublil and Jean-Marc Natel

from *Les Misérables*

Refrain:
Do you hear the people sing,
Singing the song of angry men?
It is the music of a people
Who will not be slaves again!
When the beating of your heart
Echoes the beating of the drums,
There is a life about to start
When tomorrow comes.

Will you join in our crusade?
Who will be strong and stand with me?
Beyond the barricade,
Is there a world you long to see?
Then join in the fight
That will give you the right to be free!

Refrain

Will you give all you can give,
So that our banner may advance?
Some will fall and some will live.
Will you stand up and take your chance?
The blood of the martyrs
Will water the meadows of France!

Refrain

Down in the Depths (On the Ninetieth Floor)

Words and Music by Cole Porter

from *Red, Hot and Blue!*

Manhattan—I'm up a tree,
The one I've most adored
Is bored
With me.
Manhattan, I'm awfully nice,
Nice people dine with me,
And even twice.
Yet the only one in the world I'm mad about
Talks of somebody else
And walks out.

With a million neon rainbows burning below me
And a million blazing taxis raising a roar,
Here I sit, above the town
In my pet pailletted gown.
Down in the depths on the ninetieth floor.
While the crowds at El Morocco punish the parquet,
And at "21" the couples clamor for more,
I'm deserted and depressed
In my regal eagle nest
Down in the depths on the ninetieth floor.
When the only one you wanted wants another
What's the use of swank and cash in the bank galore?
Why, even the janitor's wife
Has a perfectly good love life
And here am I
Facing tomorrow
Alone with my sorrows
Down in the depths on the ninetieth floor.

Edelweiss

Lyrics by Oscar Hammerstein II
Music by Richard Rodgers

from *The Sound of Music*

Edelweiss,
Edelweiss,
Every morning you greet me.
Small and white,
Clean and bright,
You look happy to meet me.

Blossom of snow,
May you bloom and grow,
Bloom and grow forever—

Edelweiss,
Edelweiss,
Bless my homeland forever.

Empty Chairs at Empty Tables

Music by Claude-Michel Schönberg
Lyrics by Herbert Kretzmer and Alain Boublil

from *Les Misérables*

There's a grief that can't be spoken,
There's a pain goes on and on,
Empty chairs at empty tables,
Now my friends are dead and gone.

Here they talked of revolution,
Here it was they lit the flame,
Here they sang about tomorrow,
And tomorrow never came.

From the table in the corner,
They could see a world reborn,
And they rose with voices ringing.
And I can hear them now.
The very words that they had sung
Became their last communion,
On the lonely barricade at dawn.

Oh, my friends, my friends, forgive me,
That I live, and you are gone,
There's a grief that can't be spoken,
There's a pain goes on and on.

Phantom faces at the window,
Phantom shadows on the floor.
Empty chairs at empty tables,
Where my friends will meet no more.

Oh, my friends, my friends, don't ask me
What your sacrifice was for.
Empty chairs at empty tables
Where my friends will sing no more.

Ev'ry Time We Say Goodbye

Words and Music by Cole Porter

from *Seven Lively Arts*

Ev'ry time we say goodbye
I die a little
Ev'ry time we say goodbye
I wonder why a little,
Why the gods above me
Who must be in the know
Think so little of me
They allow you to go

When you're near there's such an air
Of Spring about it,
I can hear a lark somewhere
Begin to sing about it,
There's no love song finer,
But how strange the change from major to minor
Ev'ry time we say goodbye.
Ev'ry single time
We say goodbye.

A Fellow Needs a Girl

Lyrics by Oscar Hammerstein II
Music by Richard Rodgers

from *Allegro*

A fellow needs a girl
To sit by his side
At the end of a weary day,
To sit by his side
And listen to him talk
And agree with the things he'll say.

A fellow needs a girl
To hold in his arms
When the rest of his world goes wrong,
To hold in his arms
And know that she believes
That her fellow is wise and strong.

When things go right
And his job's well done,
He wants to share
The prize he's won.
(If no one shares,
And no one cares,
Where's the fun
Of a job well done
Or a prize you've won?)

A fellow needs a home,
His own kind of home,
But to make this dream come true
A fellow needs a girl,
His own kind of girl…
My kind of girl is you.

Everybody Ought to Have a Maid

Words and Music by Stephen Sondheim

from *A Funny Thing Happened on the Way to the Forum*

Ev'rybody ought to have a maid.
(Ev'rybody ought to have a maid.)
Ev'rybody ought to have a working girl.
Ev'rybody ought to have a lurking girl,
To putter around the house.

Ev'rybody ought to have a maid.
(Ev'rybody ought to have a maid.)
Ev'rybody ought to have a menial,
Consistently congenial,
And quieter than a mouse.

Refrain:
Oh! Oh!
Wouldn't she be delicious,
Tidying up the dishes,
Neat as a pin?
Oh! Oh!
Wouldn't she be delightful,
Sweeping out?
Sleeping in?

Ev'rybody ought to have a maid!
(Ev'rybody ought to have a maid!)
Someone whom you hire when
    you're short of help,
To offer you the sort of help
You never get from a spouse.

Fluttering up the stairway,
Shuttering up the windows,
Cluttering up the bedroom,
Buttering up the master,
Puttering all around the house.

Refrain

Ev'rybody ought to have a maid.
Someone who, when fetching you your slip-
    per will
Be winsome as a whippoorwill,
And graceful as a grouse.

Skittering down the hallway,
Flittering thru the parlor,
Tittering in the pantry,
Littering up the bedroom,
Puttering all around...
The house!

ADDITIONAL LYRICS

Encore 1:
Ev'rybody ought to have a maid.
Ev'rybody ought to have a serving girl,
A loyal and unswerving girl,
Who's quieter than a mouse.

Oh! Oh!
Think of her at the dust bin,
'Specially when she's just been
Traipsing about.
Oh! Oh!
Wouldn't she be delightful,
Living in,
Giving out?

Ev'rybody ought to have a maid.
Tidily collecting bits of paper 'n' strings,
Appealing in her apron strings,
Beguiling in her blouse!

Puttering thru the attic,
Chattering in the cellar,
Clattering in the kitchen,
Flattering in the bedroom,
Puttering all around...
The house!

Encore 2:
Ev'rybody ought to have a maid.
Someone who's efficient and reliable,
Obedient and pliable,
And quieter than a mouse.

Oh! Oh!
Wouldn't she be so nimble,
Fiddling with her thimble,
Mending a gown?
Oh! Oh!
Wouldn't she be delightful,
Cleaning up,
Leaning down!

Ev'rybody ought to have a maid,
Someone who'll be busy as a bumblebee,
And even if you grumble, be
As graceful as a grouse!

Wriggling in the anteroom,
Jiggling in the living room,
Giggling in the dining room,
Wiggling in the other rooms,
Puttering all around...
The house!

Friendship

Words and Music by Cole Porter

from *DuBarry Was a Lady*

If you're ever in a jam,
Here I am.
If you're ever in a mess,
S.O.S.
If you ever feel so happy you land in jail,
I'm your bail.

It's friendship, friendship,
Just a perfect blendship.
When other friendships have been forgot,
Ours will still be hot.
Lah-dle-ah-dle-ah-dle, dig, dig, dig.

If you're ever up a tree,
'Phone to me.
If you're ever down a well,
Ring my bell.
If you ever lose your teeth and
   you're out to dine,
Borrow mine.

It's friendship, friendship,
Just a perfect blendship.
When other friendships have been forgate,
Ours will still be great.
Lah-dle-ah-dle-ah-dle, chuck, chuck, chuck.

If they ever black your eyes,
Put me wise.
If they ever cook your goose,
Turn me loose.
If they ever put a bullet through your brr-ain,
I'll complain.

It's friendship, friendship,
Just a perfect blendship.
When other friendships have been forgit,
Ours will still be it,
Lah-dle-ah-dle-ah-dle, hep, hep, hep.

ADDITIONAL LYRICS
Refrain 1:
If you're ever in a jam,
Here I am.
If you ever need a pal,
I'm your gal.
If you ever feel so happy you land in jail,
I'm your bail.

Refrain 2:
If you ever lose your way,
Come to May.
If you ever make a flop,
Call for Pop.
If you ever take a boat and get lost at sea,
Write to me.

Refrain 3:
If you're ever down a well,
Ring my bell.
If you ever catch on fire,
Send a wire.
If you ever lose your teeth and
   you're out to dine,
Borrow mine.

It's friendship, friendship,
Just a perfect blendship.
When other friendships have ceased to jell,
Ours will still be swell.
Lah-dle-ah-dle-ah-dle, hep, hep, hep.

Refrain 4:
If they ever black your eyes,
Put me wise.
If they ever cook your goose,
Turn me loose.
If they ever put a bullet
    through your brr-ain,
I'll complain.

It's friendship, friendship,
Just a perfect blendship.
When other friendships go up in smoke,
Ours will still be oke.
Lah-dle-ah-dle-ah-dle, chuck, chuck, chuck.
Gong, gong, gong,
Cluck, cluck, cluck,
Woof, woof, woof,
Peck, peck, peck,
Put, put, put,
Hip, hip, hip.
Quack, quack, quack,
Tweet, tweet, tweet,
Push, push, push,
Give, give, give.

Refrain 5:
If you ever lose your mind,
I'll be kind.
If you ever lose your shirt,
I'll be hurt.
If you're ever in a mill and
    get sawed in half,
I won't laugh.

It's friendship, friendship,
Just a perfect blendship.
When other friendships have been forgate,
Ours will still be great.
Lah-dle-ah-dle-ah-dle, goof, goof, goof.

Refrain 6:
If they ever hang you, pard,
Send a card.
If they ever cut your throat,
Write a note.
If they ever make a cannibal stew of you,
Invite me, too.

It's friendship, friendship,
Just a perfect blendship.
When other friendships are up the crick,
Ours will still be slick,
Lah-dle-ah-dle-ah-dle, zip, zip, zip.

The Gentleman Is a Dope

Lyrics by Oscar Hammerstein II
Music by Richard Rodgers

from *Allegro*

The boss gets on my nerves,
I've got a good mind to quit.
I've taken all I can,
It's time to get up and git,
And move to another job
Or maybe another town.
The gentleman burns me up,
The gentleman gets me down.

The gentleman is a dope,
A man of many faults,
A clumsy Joe
Who wouldn't know
A rhumba from a waltz.
The gentleman is a dope,
And not my cup of tea.
(Why do I get in a dither?
He doesn't belong to me.)

The gentleman isn't bright,
He doesn't know the score,
A cake will come,
He'll take a crumb
And never ask for more.
The gentleman's eyes are blue,
But little do they see.
(Why am I beating my brains out?
He doesn't belong to me.)

He's somebody else's problem,
She's welcome to the guy!
She'll never understand him
Half as well as I.

The gentleman is a dope,
He isn't very smart.
He's just a lug
You'd like to hug
And hold against your heart.
The gentleman doesn't know
How happy he could be.
(Look at me, crying my eyes out
As if he belonged to me...
He'll never belong to me.)

Getting to Know You

Lyrics by Oscar Hammerstein II
Music by Richard Rodgers

from *The King and I*

It's a very ancient saying,
But a true and honest thought,
That "if you become a teacher
By your pupils you'll be taught."
As a teacher I've been learning
(You'll forgive me if I boast)
And I've now become an expert
On the subject I like most:

Getting to know you.
Getting to know all about you,
Getting to like you,
Getting to hope you like me.
Getting to know you—
Putting it my way, but nicely,
You are precisely
My cup of tea!

Getting to know you,
Getting to feel free and easy;
When I am with you,
Getting to know what to say—
Haven't you noticed?
Suddenly I'm bright and breezy
Because of
All the beautiful and new
Things I'm learning about you,
Day by day.

Glad to Be Unhappy

Words by Lorenz Hart
Music by Richard Rodgers

from *On Your Toes*

Look at yourself.
If you had a sense of humor,
You would laugh to beat the band.
Look at yourself.
Do you still believe the rumor
That romance is simply grand?
Since you took it right on the chin,
You have lost that bright toothpaste grin.
My mental state is all a jumble.
I sit around and sadly mumble.

Refrain:
Fools rush in, so here I am,
Very glad to be unhappy.
I can't win, but here I am,
More than glad to be unhappy.
Unrequited love's a bore,
And I've got it pretty bad.
But for someone you adore,
It's a pleasure to be sad.
Like a straying baby lamb
With no mammy and no pappy,
I'm so unhappy, but oh, so glad.

Gonna Build a Mountain

Words and Music by Leslie Bricusse and Anthony Newley

from the Musical Production *Stop the World—I Want to Get Off*

Gonna build a mountain from a little hill.
Gonna build a mountain, least I hope I will.
Gonna build a mountain; gonna build it high.
I don't know how I'm gonna do it;
Only know I'm gonna try.

Gonna build a daydream from a little hope.
Gonna push that daydream up the mountain slope.
Gonna build a daydream; gonna see it through.
Gonna build a mountain and a daydream;
Gonna make 'em both come true.

Gonna build a heaven from a little hell.
Gonna build a heaven and I know darn well.
If I build my mountain with a lot of care.
And take my daydream up the mountain
Heaven will be waiting there.

When I've built that heaven, as I will someday,
And the Lord sends Gabriel to take me away,
Wanna a fine young son to take my place.
I'll leave a son in my heaven on earth,
With the Lord's good grace.

With a fine young son to take my place
I'll leave a son in my heaven on earth
With the Lord's good grace.

Guys and Dolls

By Frank Loesser

from *Guys and Dolls*

What's playing at the Roxy?
I'll tell you what's playing at the Roxy.
A picture about a Minnesota man,
So in love with a Mississippi girl
That he sacrifices everything
And moves all the way to Biloxi.
That's what's playing at the Roxy.

What's in the Daily News?
I'll tell you what's in the Daily News,
Story about a guy
Who bought his wife a small ruby,
With what otherwise would have been
His union dues.
That's what's in the Daily News.

What's happening all over?
I'll tell you what's happening all over.
Guys sitting home by a television set,
Who once used to be something of a rover,
That's what's happening all over.
Love is the thing that has lick'd 'em.
And it looks like Nathan's
    just another victim.
(Spoken) Yes sir!

When you see a guy reach for
    stars in the sky,
You can bet that he's doing it for some doll.
When you spot a John waiting
    out in the rain,
Chances are he's insane as only a John
Can be for a Jane.

When you meet a gent paying all kinds of rent,
For a flat that could flatten the Taj Mahal,
Call it sad, call it funny,
But it's better than even money,
That the guy's only doing it for some doll.

When you see a Joe saving half of his dough,
You can bet there'll be mink in it for some doll,
When a bum buys wine like a bum can't afford,
It's a cinch that the bum is under the thumb
Of some little broad.

When you meet a mugg lately out of the jug,
And he's still lifting platinum folderol,
Call it hell, call it heaven,
It's a probable twelve to seven,
That the guy's only doing it for some doll.

When you see a sport and his cash has
    run short,
Make a bet that he's banking it with some doll.
When a guy wears tails with the
    front gleaming white,
Who the hell do you think he's tickling pink
On Saturday night?

When a lazy slob takes a good steady job,
And he smells from Vitalis and Barbasol,
Call it dumb, call it clever,
Ah, but you can give it odds forever,
That the guy's only doing it for some doll,
Some doll, some doll,
The guy's only doing it for some doll.

Haben Sie Gehört Das Deutsche Band?
(Have You Ever Heard the German Band?)

Music and Lyrics by Mel Brooks

from *The Producers*

Haben Sie gehört das Deutsche band?
Mit a bang,
Mit a boom,
Mit a bing bang bing bang boom!

Haben Sie gehört das Deutsche band?
Mit a bang,
Mit a boom,
Mit a bing bang bing bang boom!

Russian folksongs
And French oo-la-la
Can't compare
With that German oom-pah-pah!

Refrain:
Ve're sayin',
Haben Sie gehört das Deutsche band?
Mit a zetz,
Mit a zap,
Mit a zing!

Polish polkas,
They're stupid und they're rotten!

Spoken:
It don't mean a thing
If it ain't got that
Schweigen Reigen
Schönen Schützen
Schmützen Sauerbraten.
Key change!

Refrain

It's the only kind of music that ve huns,
And our honeys love to sing!
(Spoken) Haben Sie gehört!

Happiness

Words and Music by Clark Gesner

from *You're a Good Man, Charlie Brown*

Happiness is two kinds of ice cream,
Finding your skate key,
Telling the time.

Happiness is learning to whistle,
Tying your shoe,
For the very first time.

Happiness is playing the drum
In your own school band.
And happiness is walking,
Hand in hand.

Happiness is finding a nickel,
Catching a firefly,
Setting him free.

Happiness is being alone,
Ev'ry now and then.
And happiness is coming home,
Again.

Happiness is having a sister,
Sharing a sandwich,
Getting along.

Happiness is singing together,
When day is through.
And happiness is those
Who sing with you.

Happiness is morning and evening,
Daytime and nighttime, too,
For happiness is anyone,
And anything at all
That's loved by you.

Have You Met Miss Jones?

Words by Lorenz Hart
Music by Richard Rodgers

from *I'd Rather Be Right*

It happened, I felt it happen.
I was awake, I wasn't blind.
I didn't think, I felt it happen.
Now I believe in matter over mind.
And you see we mustn't wait.
The nearest moment that we marry is too late!

"Have you met Miss Jones?"
Someone said as we shook hands.
She was just Miss Jones to me.
Then I said, "Miss Jones,
You're a girl who understands
I'm a man who must be free."
And all at once I lost my breath.
And all at once was scared to death.
And all at once I owned the earth and sky!
Now I've met Miss Jones
And we'll keep on meeting till we die,
Miss Jones and I.

He Was Too Good to Me

Words by Lorenz Hart
Music by Richard Rodgers

from *Simple Simon*

There goes my young intended.
The thing is ended.
Regrets are vain.
I'll never find another half so sweet
And we'll never meet again.

I was a good sport,
Told him
Goodbye.
Eyes dim,
But why complain?

He was too good to me
How can I get along now?
So close he stood to me
Everything seems all wrong now.
He would have brought me the sun.
Making me smile,
That was his fun.
When I was mean to him,
He'd never say, "Go 'way now."
I was a queen to him.
Who's goin' to make me gay now?
It's only natural I'm blue.
He was too good to be true.

Heat Wave

Words and Music by Irving Berlin

from the Stage Production *As Thousands Cheer*

A heat wave blew right into town last week.
She came from the Island of Martinique.
The can-can she dances will make you fry.
The can-can is really the reason why.

Refrain:
We're having a heat wave,
A tropical heat wave.
The temperature's rising,
It isn't surprising.
She certainly can can-can.
She started a heat wave
By letting her seat wave.
And in such a way that
The customers say that
She certainly can can-can.
Gee her anatomy
Made the mercury
Jump to ninety-three.
Yes sir!
We're having a heat wave
A tropical heat wave,
The way that she moves
That thermometer proves
That she certainly can can-can.

Repeat Refrain

Patter:
It's so hot the weather man
Will tell you a record's been made.
It's so hot a coat of tan
Will cover your face in the shade.
It's so hot the coldest maiden
Feels just as warm as a bride.
It's so hot a chicken laid an
Egg on the street and it fried.

Refrain

The Hostess with the Mostes' on the Ball

Words and Music by Irving Berlin

from the Stage Production *Call Me Madam*

I was born on a thousand acres
Of Oklahoma land,
Nothing grew on the thousand acres,
For it was gravel and sand.
One day father started digging in a field,
Hoping to find some soil.
He dug and he dug, and what do you think?
Oil, oil, oil.
The money rolled in and I rolled out,
With a fortune piled so high.
Washington was my destination,
And now, who am I?

I'm the chosen party giver
For the White House clientele,
And they know that I deliver
What it takes to make 'em jell.
And in Washington, I'm known by
    one and all
As the hostess with the mostes' on the ball.

They would go to Elsa Maxwell,
When they had an axe to grind,
They could always grind their axe well,
At the parties she designed.
Now the hatchet grinders all prefer to call,
On the hostess with the mostes' on the ball.

I've a great big bar,
And good caviar,
Yes the best that can be found,
And a large amount
In my bank account,
When election time comes 'round.

If you're feeling presidential,
You can make it, yes, indeed,
There are just three things essential,
Let me tell you all you need,
Is an ounce of wisdom and a pound of gall,
And the hostess with the mostes' on the ball.

An Ambassador has just reached the shore,
He's a man of many loves.
An important gent from the Orient,
To be handled with kid gloves,
He can come and let his hair down,
Have the best time of his life,
Even bring his new affair down,
Introduce her as his wife,
But she mustn't leave her panties in the hall.
For the hostess who's the hostess,
With the mostes' on the ball.

ADDITIONAL LYRICS
Encore:
I've been highly complimented,
And I thank you what is more,
You'll be damned well represented
By your new ambassador,
For my one ambition is to make them fall,
For the hostess with the mostes' on the ball.

In the handbag that I'll carry,
There's a precious little note,
To their highnesses from Harry,
Introducing me, he wrote,
I'll appreciate a favour, large or small,
For the hostess with the mostes' on the ball.

There'll be no mistakes,
I've got what it takes,
To make friends across the sea.
I'll make being smart
An important part
Of my foreign policy.

I'll cement our good relations,
When I give my first affair.
There'll be special invitations
To the Duke and Duchess there,
Who's already written asking them to call,
Not the priestess with the leastes',
But the hostess with the mostes',
With the mostes' on the ball.

I Ain't Down Yet

By Meredith Willson

from *The Unsinkable Molly Brown*

Spoken:
Now looka here—
I am important to me!
I ain't no bottom to no pile.
I mean much more to me
Than I mean to anybody I ever knew!
Certainly more than I mean to any
Si-wash yazzi-hampers like you guys.
Go ahead! Break muh arm!
Me say Uncle? Heh!
Doesn't make a bit-a diff'rence
For you to keep sayin' I'm down, till
Sung:
I say so, too.

Spoken:
J'ever try steppin' on a pissant?
Well, there's one now!
Jump him! Stomp him!
You thinkin' you got him?
Thinkin' he's quit?
Well, he don't think so.
There he goes!
And you can be positive sure,
I'm as good as any pissant that ever lived!
Oh, I hate that word "down,"
But I love the word "up,"
'Cause "up" means hope
An' that's just what I got.
Hope for some place better,
Some place—I dunno—
Cleaner, shinier.

Hell, if I gotta eat catfish heads all my life,
Can't I have 'em offa plate once?
And a red silk dress,
Sung:
When there's girl enough on me to wear one.
And then, someday,
With all my might and all my main,
I'm goan' to:

Learn to read and write.
I'm goan' to see what there is to see.
So, if you go from nowhere
On the road to somewhere,
And you meet anyone,
You'll know it's me.

Spoken:
I'm goan' to
Sung:
Move from place to place,
To find a house with a golden stair.
And if that house is red,
And has a big brass bed,
I'm livin' there!

I Am What I Am

Music and Lyric by Jerry Herman

from *La Cage Aux Folles*

I am what I am,
I am my own
Special creation,
So, come take a look,
Give me the hook,
Or the ovation.

It's my world,
That I want to have a little pride in,
My world,
And it's not a place I have to hide in.

Refrain:
Life's not worth a damn,
'Til you can say, "Hey world,
I am what I am."

I am what I am,
I don't want praise,
I don't want pity.
I bang my own drum,
Some think it's noise,
I think it's pretty.

And so what,
If I love each feather and each spangle,
Why not
Try and see things from a diff'rent angle?
[Or:]
It's my song,
And if you don't like the style I bring it,
My song,
So at least respect my right to sing it.

Your life is a sham,
'Til you can shout out loud,
"I am what I am."

I am what I am,
And what I am
Needs no excuses,
I deal my own deck,
Sometimes the ace,
Sometimes the deuces.

There's one life,
And there's no return and no deposit,
One life,
So it's time to open up your closet.
[Or:]
It's high time
That I blow my horn and sound my trumpet.
High time,
And if you don't like it, you can lump it.

Refrain

I Believe in You

By Frank Loesser

from the musical *How to Succeed in Business Without Really Trying*

You have the cool clear eyes
Of a seeker of wisdom and truth,
Yet, there's that up turned chin
And the grin of impetuous youth.
Oh, I believe in you,
I believe in you.

I hear the sound of good
Solid judgment whenever you talk,
Yet, there's the bold, brave spring
Of the tiger that quickens your walk.
Oh, I believe in you,
I believe in you.

And when my faith in my fellow man
All but falls apart,
I've but to feel your hand grasping mine
And I take heart,
I take heart.

To see the cool clear eyes
Of a seeker of wisdom and truth,
Yet there's that slam bang tang
Reminiscent of gin and vermouth.
Oh, I believe in you,
I believe in you.

I Can't Get Started with You

Words by Ira Gershwin
Music by Vernon Duke

from the musical *Ziegfeld Follies* (1936)

I've flown around the world in a plane;
I've settled revolutions in Spain;
The North Pole I have charted,
But I can't get started with you.

Around the golf course I'm under par,
And all the movies want me to star;
I've got a home, a showplace,
But I get no-place with you.

You're so supreme,
Lyrics I write of you, scheme,
Just for a sight of you, dream,
Both day and night of you
And what good does it do?

In nineteen twenty-nine I sold short,
In England I'm presented at court,
But you've got me down-hearted
'Cause I can't get started with you.

I do a hundred yards in ten flat;
The Prince of Wales has copied my hat;
With queens I've a-la carted,
But can't get started with you.

The leading tailors follow my styles,
And toothpaste ads all feature my smiles;
The Astor-bilts I visit,
But say, what is it with you?

When we first met,
How you elated me! Pet,
You devastated me! Yet,
Now you've deflated me
'Til you're my Waterloo.

I've sold my kisses at a bazaar
And after me they've named a cigar;
But lately how I've smarted,
'Cause I can't get started with you.

I Can't Give You Anything but Love

By Jimmy McHugh and Dorothy Fields

from *Blackbirds of 1928*

I can't give you anything but love, Baby,
That's the only thing I've plenty of, Baby.
Dreamin' a while,
Schemin' a while,
You're sure to find,
Happiness an' I guess,
All those things you've always pined for.
Gee, I'd like to see you lookin' swell, Baby,
Diamond bracelets Woolworth doesn't sell, Baby.
Till that lucky day you know darn well.
I can't give you anything but love.
I can't give you anything but love.

I Could Write a Book

Words by Lorenz Hart
Music by Richard Rodgers

from *Pal Joey*

A B C D E F G
I never learned to spell,
At least not well.
1 2 3 4 5 6 7
I never learned to count
A great amount.
But my busy mind is burning
To use what learning I've got.
I won't waste any time,
I'll strike while the iron is hot.

Refrain:
If they asked me, I could write a book
About the way you walk and whisper and look.
I could write a preface on how we met
So the world would never forget.
And the simple secret of the plot
Is just to tell them that I love you a lot.
Then the world discovers as my book ends
How to make two lovers of friends.

Used to hate to go to school.
I never cracked a book;
I played the hook.
Never answered any mail;
To write I used to think
Was wasting ink.
It was never my endeavor
To be too clever and smart.
Now I suddenly feel
A longing to write in my heart.

Refrain

I Found a Million Dollar Baby
(In a Five and Ten Cent Store)

Lyric by Billy Rose and Mort Dixon
Music by Harry Warren

from *Crazy Quilt*

Verse:
Love comes along like a popular song,
Anytime or anywhere at all.
Rain or sunshine, spring or fall,
You never know when it may say hello
In a very unexpected place
For example, take my case:

Refrain 1:
It was a lucky April shower,
It was the most convenient door;
I found a million dollar baby
In a five and ten cent store.

Refrain 2:
The rain continued for an hour,
I hung around for three or four,
Around a million dollar baby
In a five and ten cent store.

Refrain 3:
She was selling china
And when she made those eyes
I kept buying china
Until the crowd got wise.

Refrain 4:
Incidentally, if you run into a shower,
Just step inside my cottage door
And meet the million dollar baby
From the five and ten cent store!

Love used to be quite a stranger to me
Didn't know a sentimental word,
Thoughts of kissing seemed absurd.
Then came a change, and you may
    think it strange,
But the world became a happy tune
Since that April afternoon.

Repeat Refrains

I Got the Sun in the Morning

Words and Music by Irving Berlin

from the Stage Production *Annie Get Your Gun*

Taking stock of what I have and what I haven't,
What do I find?
The things I've got will keep me satisfied.

Checking up on what I have and what I haven't,
What do I find?
A healthy balance on the credit side.

Got no diamond,
Got no pearl,
Still I think I'm a lucky girl.
I got the sun in the morning and the moon at night.

Got no mansion,
Got no yacht,
Still I'm happy with what I've got.
I got the sun in the morning and the moon at night.

Sunshine
Gives me a lovely day.
Moonlight
Gives me the Milky Way.

Got no check books,
Got no banks,
Still I'd like to express my thanks.
I got the sun in the morning and the moon at night.

And with the sun in the morning
And the moon in the evening,
I'm all right.

I Hate You, Darling

Words and Music by Cole Porter

from *Let's Face It*

I hate you, darling,
My turtle dove,
I hate you, darling,
All else above,
I hate you, darling,
Because I love you so.

I should be clever
And say, "Goodbye,"
Goodbye, forever,
My butterfly.
But why be clever,
When darling I need
The joy you bring me,
More than anything I know.

I'm in the depths of Inferno
When you're far away from me, dear.
But when our sweet nights return,
Oh, my habitat is the stratosphere.

Still I hate you, darling,
It's true my pet,
I hate you, darling,
But don't forget,
I hate you, darling,
And yet, I love you so.

I Have Dreamed

Lyrics by Oscar Hammerstein II
Music by Richard Rodgers

from *The King and I*

I have dreamed that your arms are lovely.
I have dreamed what a joy you'll be.
I have dreamed every word you'll whisper
When you're close, close to me.

How you look in the glow of evening,
I have dreamed and enjoyed the view.
In these dreams I've loved you so
That by now I think I know
What it's like to be loved by you.
I will love being loved by you.

I Love My Wife

Words by Tom Jones
Music by Harvey Schmidt

from *I Do! I Do!*

He:
I love my wife.
What should I do?
I've been to see a specialist,
But when he was through,
He told me it's hopeless,
I'm stricken for life.
"My son," he said, "Get back to bed.
You happen to love your wife."

Other men love famous stars,
But, not I,
The sort you worship from afar,
And I try.
Other men love femmes fatales,
Sveltely dressed.
But when I'm with those femmes fatales,
I get depressed,
'Cause,

Refrain:
I love my wife.
How will it end?
I love her as a lover and not
Just as a friend.
It may be abnormal.
With drama it's rife.
But nevertheless,
I confess I love my wife!

Spoken:
Agnes!
Agnes, wake up!
Sung:
Uh—uh—uh—

She (Spoken):
Michael, what are you doing?
He (Spoken):
I'm pushing you around in the bed.
(Sung:)
I love Agnes!
She (Spoken):
I love you, too.
But have you gone completely batty?
He (Spoken):
Mmm-hmmm.
(Sung:)
I love Agnes.
She (Spoken):
I'm getting dizzy.
He (Sung):
So am I.

Refrain

Nevertheless, I confess I love my wife.
I love my wife.
I love my wife.
Doodle, oodle, oodle, oodle,
   doo—doo—doo.
(Spoken:) I adore my wife!

I Love Paris

Words and Music by Cole Porter

from *Can-Can*

Ev'ry time I look down
On this timeless town,
Whether blue or grey be her skies,
Whether loud be her cheers
Or whether soft be her tears,
More and more do I realize.

I love Paris in the springtime,
I love Paris in the fall.
I love Paris in the winter, when it drizzles,
I love Paris in the summer, when it sizzles.

I love Paris ev'ry moment,
Ev'ry moment of the year,
I love Paris,
Why, oh why do I love Paris?
Because my love is near.

I Love You

Words and Music by Cole Porter

from *Mexican Hayride*

If a love song I could only write,
A song with words and music divine,
I would serenade you ev'ry night,
Till you'd relent and consent to be mine.

But alas, just an amateur am I,
And so I'll not be surprised, my dear,
If you smile and politely pass it by,
When this, my first love song, you hear.

"I love you,"
Hums the April breeze,
"I love you,"
Echo the hills.
"I love you,"
The golden dawn agrees,
As once more she sees
Daffodils.

It's spring again,
And birds on the wing again
Start to sing again,
The old melodie.

"I love you,"
That's the song of songs,
And it all belongs
To you and me.

I Loved You Once in Silence

Words by Alan Jay Lerner
Music by Frederick Loewe

from *Camelot*

I loved you once in silence,
And mis'ry was all I knew.
Trying so to keep my love from showing,
All the while not knowing
You loved me too.

Yes, loved me in lonesome silence,
Your heart filled with dark despair,
Thinking love would flame in you forever,
And I'd never, never
Know the flame was there.

Then one day we cast away
Our secret longing,
The raging tide we held inside
Would hold no more.

The silence at last was broken!
We flung wide our prison door.
Ev'ry joyous word of love was spoken,
And now there's twice as much grief,
Twice the strain for us,
Twice the despair,
Twice the pain for us
As we had known before.

I Never Has Seen Snow

Lyric by Truman Capote and Harold Arlen
Music by Harold Arlen

from *House of Flowers*

I done lost my ugly spell,
I am cheerful now.
Got the warm all-overs
A-smoothin' my worried brow.
Oh, the girl I used to be,
She ain't me no more,
I closed the door
On the girl I was before.
Feelin' fine and full o' bliss,
What I really wants to say is this.

I never has seen snow,
All the same I know,
Snow ain't so beautiful,
C'ain't be so beautiful
Like my love is,
Like my love is.

Nothin' do compare,
Nothin' anywhere,
With my love.

A hundred things I see,
A twilight sky that's free,
But none so beautiful,
Not one so beautiful,
Like my love is,
Like my love is.

Once you see his face,
None can take the place
Of my love.

A stone rolled off my heart
When I laid my eyes on
That near-to-me boy,
With that far away look,
And right from the start,
I saw a new horizon
And a road to take me
Where I wanted to be took,
Needed to be took.

And though,
I never has seen snow,
All the same I know
Nothin' will ever be,
Nothin' can ever be
Beautiful as my love is,
Like my love is,
To me.

I Still Believe in Love

Words by Carole Bayer Sager
Music by Marvin Hamlisch

from *They're Playing Our Song*

After all the tears I cried,
You'd think I would give up on love,
Get off that line,
But maybe I can get it right this time.

I was there as passion turned to pain,
Sunshine turned to rainy days,
Yet here I am,
Ready to begin once again.

All my life I've been a dreamer,
Dreaming dreams that never quite come true,
But I still believe in love,
And love believin',
Maybe you can make my dreams come true.

Here, content with who I am,
I'm reachin' out my hand to him [her],
Once again,
At least I know I made myself a friend.

All my life I've been a dreamer,
Dreaming dreams that always broke in two.
But I still believe in love,
And love believin',
I'll keep on dreamin' because I still believe in love.
I still believe in love,
And me and you,
I still believe in love.

I Went to a Marvelous Party

Words and Music by Noel Coward

from *Set to Music*

Quite for no reason
I'm here for the season,
And high as a kite.
Living in error
With Maude at Cap Farrat,
Which couldn't be right.

Ev'ryone's here and frightf'lly gay,
Nobody cares what people say,
Tho' the Riviera
Seems really much queerer
Than Rome at its height.
Yesterday night—

Refrain:
I've been to a marvelous party,
I must say the fun was intense,
We all had to do what the people we knew
Would be doing a hundred years hence.
Dear Cecil arrived wearing armour,
Some shells and a black feather boa.
Poor Millicent wore a surrealist comb,
Made of bits of Mosaic from St. Peter's in Rome,
But the weight was so great that she had to go home,
I couldn't have liked it more!

Refrain

I'd Give My Life for You

Music by Claude-Michel Schönberg
Lyrics by Richard Maltby Jr. and Alain Boublil
Adapted from original French Lyrics by Alain Boublil

from *Miss Saigon*

You, who I cradled in my arms,
You, asking as little as you can.
Little snip of a little man.
I know I'd give my life for you.

You didn't ask me to be born, you.
Why should you learn of war or pain?
To make sure you're not hurt again,
I swear I'd give my life for you.

I've tasted love beyond all fear.
And you should know it's love
That brought you here.
And in one perfect night,
When the stars burned like new,
I knew what I must do.

I'll give you a million things
I'll never own,
I'll give you a world to conquer
When you're grown.

Refrain:
You will be who you want to be.
You can choose whatever heaven grants.
As long as you can have your chance,
I swear I'd give my life for you.

Sometimes I wake up reaching for him.
I feel his shadow brush my head,
But there's just moonlight on my bed.
Was he a ghost? Was he a lie?
That made my body laugh and cry?
Then by my side the proof I see:
His little one. Gods of the sun,
Bring him to me!

Refrain

No one can stop what I must do.
I swear I'll give my life for you!

Music and Lyrics Copyright © 1987 by Alain Boublil Music Ltd. (ASCAP)
English Lyrics Copyright © 1988 by Alain Boublil Music Ltd. (ASCAP)
Additional Music and English Lyrics Copyright © 1989 and 1991 by
    Alain Boublil Music Ltd. (ASCAP)
Mechanical and Publication Rights for the U.S.A. Administered by
    Alain Boublil Music Ltd. (ASCAP) c/o Stephen Tenenbaum & Co., Inc.,
    1775 Broadway, Suite 708, New York, NY 10019, Tel. (212) 246-7204,
    Fax (212) 246-7217

I'll Know

By Frank Loesser

from *Guys and Dolls*

Sarah:
For I've imagined ev'ry bit of him,
From his strong moral fibre,
To the wisdom in his head,
To the homey aroma of his pipe.

Sky:
You have wished yourself
A Scarsdale Galahad,
The breakfast eating,
Brooks Brothers type!

Sarah (Spoken):
Yes.
(Sung):
And I shall meet him
When the time is ripe.

I'll know when my love comes along,
I won't take a chance.
For oh, he'll be just what I need,
Not some fly-by-night Broadway romance.

Sky:
And you'll know at a glance
By the two pair of pants.

Sarah:
I'll know by the calm steady voice,
Those feet on the ground,
I'll know as I run to his arms,
That at last I've come home safe and sound.

And till then,
I shall wait,
And till then, I'll be strong.
For I'll know when my love comes along.

Sky:
Mine will come as a surprise to me,
Mine, I leave to chance,
And chemistry.
Sarah (Spoken):
Chemistry?
Sky (Spoken):
Yes, chemistry.

Suddenly I'll know when my love
    comes along,
I'll know then and there,
I'll know at the sight of her face.
How I care, how I care, how I care!

And I'll stop,
And I'll stare.
And I'll know, long before we can speak,
I'll know in my heart,
I'll know, and I won't ever ask,
"Am I right? Am I wise? Am I smart?"

But I'll stop,
And I'll stare,
At that face in the throng,
Yes, I'll know when my love comes along.
Sarah:
I'll know.
Both:
When my love comes along

ADDITIONAL LYRICS
Sarah:
I won't take a chance,
My love will be just what I need,
Not some fly-by-night Broadway romance,
And till then,
I shall wait,
And till then, I'll be strong.
For I'll know when my love comes along.

I'll Never Fall in Love Again

Lyric by Hal David
Music by Burt Bacharach

from *Promises, Promises*

What do you get when you fall in love,
A girl {guy} with a pin to burst your bubble,
That's what you get for all your trouble,
I'll never fall in love again.
I'll never fall in love again.

What do you get when you kiss a girl {guy},
You get enough germs to catch pneumonia,
After you do, she'll {he'll} never phone you;
I'll never fall in love again.

Refrain:
I'll never fall in love again.
Don't tell me what it's all about,
'Cause I've been there and I'm glad I'm out;
Out of those chains, those chains that
   bind you,
That is why I'm here to remind you.
What do you get when you fall in love,
You only get lies and pain and sorrow,
So for at least until tomorrow,
I'll never fall in love again,
I'll never fall in love again.

What do you get when you give your heart,
You get it all broken up and battered,
That's what you get, a heart that's tattered;
I'll never fall in love again.

Refrain

What do you get when you need a girl {guy},
You get enough tears to fill an ocean,
That's what you get for your devotion;
I'll never fall in love again.

Refrain

I'll Never Say No

By Meredith Willson

from *The Unsinkable Molly Brown*

I'll never say no to you,
Whatever you say or do.
If you ask me to wait
For a lifetime,
You know I'll gladly wait
For a lifetime or two,
Just to look at you.

Refrain:
I'll smile when you say, "Be glad."
I'll weep if you want me sad.
Today is tomorrow,
If you want it so,
I'll stay or I'll go,
But I'll never say no.

Refrain

I'm Flying

Lyric by Carolyn Leigh
Music by Mark Charlap

from *Peter Pan*

I'm flying.
Look at me, way up high,
Suddenly, here am I,
I'm flying.

I'm flying.
I can soar; I can weave,
And what's more,
I'm not even trying.

High up and as light
As I can be.
I must be a sight
Lovely to see.

I'm flying.
Nothing will stop me now,
Higher still, look at how
I can zoom around,
'Way up off the ground,
I'm flying.

I'm flying.
Like an owl, like a bat
On the prowl,
It's so satisfying.

I'm whizzin',
Through a cloud, past a star,
I'm so proud,
Look how far I've risen.

High over the moon,
Higher I fly.
'Bye old mister moon,
Bid me goodbye.

I'm flying.
Heading far out of sight,
Second star to the right,
Now the way is clear,
Neverland is near.
Follow all the arrows,
I'm about to disappear,
I'm flying.

I'm Glad I'm Not Young Anymore

Words by Alan Jay Lerner
Music by Frederick Loewe

from *Gigi*

Poor boy, poor boy,
Downhearted and depressed and in a spin.
Poor boy, poor boy,
Oh, youth can really do a fellow in.

How lovely to sit here in the shade,
With none of the woes of man and maid,
I'm glad I'm not young anymore.
The rivals that don't exist at all,
The feeling you're only two feet tall,
I'm glad that I'm not young anymore.

No more confusion,
No "morning after" surprise,
No self-delusion
That when you're telling those lies,
She isn't wise.

And even if love comes thru the door,
The kind that goes on forevermore,
Forevermore is shorter than before.
Oh, I'm so glad that I'm not young anymore.

The tiny remark that tortures you,
The fear that your friends won't
   like her too,
I'm glad I'm not young anymore.
The longing to end a stale affair,
Until you find out she doesn't care,
I'm glad that I'm not young anymore.

No more frustration,
No star-crossed lover am I,
No aggravation,
Just one reluctant reply,
"Lady, goodbye."

The fountain of youth is dull as paint,
Methuselah is my patron saint,
I've never been so comfortable before.
Oh, I'm so glad that I'm not young anymore.

I'm Still Here

Words and Music by Stephen Sondheim

from *Follies*

*Note: The lyrics have been revised in subsequent versions;
these are the original show lyrics.*

Good times and bum times,
I've seen them all and, my dear,
I'm still here.
Plush velvet sometimes,
Sometimes just pretzels and beer,
But I'm here.
I've stuffed the dailies in my shoes,
Strummed ukuleles, sung the blues,
Seen all my dreams disappear,
But I'm here.

I've slept in shanties,
Guest of the W.P.A.
But I'm here.
Danced in my scanties,
Three bucks a night was the pay,
But I'm here.
I've stood on breadlines with the best,
Watched while the headlines did the rest.
In the depression was I depressed?
Nowhere near.
I met a big financier and I'm here.

I've been through Ghandi,
Windsor and Wally's affair,
And I'm here.
Amos 'n' Andy
Mahjongg and platinum hair,
And I'm here.
I got through Abie's Irish Rose,
Five Dionne babes, Major Bowes,
Had heebie jeebies for Beebe's Bathysphere.
I lived through Brenda Frazier, and I'm here.

I've gotten through Herbert and
    J. Edgar Hoover,
Gee, that was fun and a half.
When you've been through Herbert and
    J. Edgar Hoover,
Anything else is a laugh.

I've been through Reno,
I've been through Beverly Hills,
And I'm here.
Reefers and vino,
Rest cures, religion and pills,
And I'm here.
Been called a pinko Commie tool,
Got through it stinko by my pool.
I should have gone to an acting school,
That seems clear.
Still, someone said, "She's sincere,"
So I'm here.

Black sable one day,
Next day it goes into hock.
But I'm here.
Top billing Monday,
Tuesday you're touring in stock,
But I'm here.
First you're another sloe-eyed vamp,
Then someone's mother,
Then you're camp.
Then you career from career to career.
I'm almost through my memoirs
And I'm here.

I've gotten through "Hey lady aren't
    you whoozis?
Wow! What a looker you were."
Or better yet, "Sorry, I thought
    you were whoozis,
Whatever happened to her?"

Good times and bum times,
I've seen 'em all my dear,
I'm still here.
Plush velvet sometimes,
Sometimes just pretzels and beer,
But I'm here.
I've run the gamut, A to Z.
Three cheers and dammit, c'est la vie.
I got through all of last year.
And I'm here.
Lord knows, at least I was there,
And I'm here!
Look who's here!
I'm still here!

If Ever I Would Leave You

Words by Alan Jay Lerner
Music by Frederick Loewe

from *Camelot*

If ever I would leave you
It wouldn't be in summer.
Seeing you in summer
I never would go.
Your hair streaked with sunlight,
Your lips red as flame,
Your face with a luster
That puts gold to shame!

But if I'd ever leave you,
It couldn't be in autumn,
How I'd leave in autumn
I never will know.
I've seen how you sparkle
When fall nips the air.
I know you in autumn
And I must be there.

And could I leave you running merrily through the snow?
Or on a wintry evening when you catch the fire's glow?

If ever I would leave you,
How could it be in springtime,
Knowing how in spring I'm bewitched by you so?
Oh, no! Not in springtime,
Summer, winter or fall!
No, never could I leave you at all.

If He Walked into My Life

Music and Lyric by Jerry Herman

from *Mame*

Where's that boy with the bugle?
My little love,
Who was always my big romance.
Where's that boy with the bugle?
And why did I ever
Buy him those damn long pants?

Did he need a stronger hand?
Did he need a lighter touch?
Was I soft or was I tough?
Did I give enough?
Did I give too much?
At the moment when he needed me,
Did I ever turn away?
Would I be there when he called,
If he walked into my life today?

Were his days a little dull?
Were his nights a little wild?
Did I overstate my plan?
Did I stress the man,
And forget the child?
And there must have been a million things
That my heart forgot to say.
Would I think of one or two,
If he walked into my life today?

Should I blame the times I pampered him?
Or blame the times I bossed him?
What a shame I never really found
The boy before I lost him.

Were the years a little fast?
Was his world a little free?
Was there too much of a crowd?
All too lush and loud,
And not enough of me?
Tho' I'll ask myself my whole life long,
What went wrong along the way?
Would I make the same mistakes
If he walked into my life, today?
If that boy with the bugle
Walked into my life, today?

If I Loved You

Lyrics by Oscar Hammerstein II
Music by Richard Rodgers

from *Carousel*

If I loved you,
Time and again I would try to say
All I'd want you to know.
If I loved you,
Words wouldn't come in an easy way,
'Round in circles I'd go.
Longin' to tell you, but afraid and shy,
I'd let my golden chances pass me by!
Soon you'd leave me,
Off you would go in the mist of day,
Never, never to know
How I loved you,
If I loved you.

The Impossible Dream (The Quest)

Lyric by Joe Darion
Music by Mitch Leigh

from *Man of La Mancha*

To dream the impossible dream,
To fight the unbeatable foe,
To bear with unbearable sorrow,
To run where the brave dare not go.

To right the unrightable wrong,
To love pure and chaste from afar,
To try when your arms are too weary,
To reach the unreachable star!

This is my quest,
To follow that star,
No matter how hopeless,
No matter how far;
To fight for the right
Without question or pause.
To be willing to march into hell for a heavenly cause!

And I know,
If I'll only be true
To this glorious quest,
That my heart
Will lie peaceful and calm,
When I'm laid to my rest,

And the world will be better for this;
That one man, scorned and covered with scars,
Still strove with his last ounce of courage,
To reach the unreachable stars.

In Buddy's Eyes (Buddy's There)

Words and Music by Stephen Sondheim

from *Follies*

Life is slow but it seems exciting,
'Cause Buddy's there.
Gourmet cooking and letter writing
And knowing Buddy's there.

Ev'ry morning,
Don't faint, I tend the flowers.
Can you believe it?
Ev'ry weekend ,
I paint for umpteen hours.
And yes, I miss a lot,
Living like a shut-in.
No, I haven't got
Cooks and cars and diamonds.
Yes, my clothes are not
Paris fashions, but in
Buddy's eyes,
I'm young, I'm beautiful.
In Buddy's eyes,
I don't get older.
So life is ducky and time goes flying,
And I'm so lucky I feel like crying and…

In Buddy's eyes,
I'm young, I'm beautiful,
In Buddy's eyes,
I can't get older.
I'm still the princess,
Still the prize.

In Buddy's eyes,
I'm young, I'm beautiful.
In Buddy's arms,
On Buddy's shoulder,
I won't get older.
Nothing dies.

And all I ever dreamed I'd be,
The best I ever thought of me,
Is ev'ry minute there to see,
In Buddy's eyes.

It Might as Well Be Spring

Lyrics by Oscar Hammerstein II
Music by Richard Rodgers

from *State Fair*

I'm as restless as a willow in a windstorm.
I'm as jumpy as a puppet on a string!
I'd say that I had spring fever,
But I know it isn't spring.
I am starry-eyed and vaguely discontented,
Like a nightingale without a song to sing.
Oh, why should I have spring fever
When it isn't even spring?

I keep wishing I were somewhere else,
Walking down a strange new street,
Hearing words that I have never heard
From a man I've yet to meet.

I'm as busy as a spider, spinning daydreams,
I'm as giddy as a baby on a swing.
I haven't seen a crocus or a rosebud
Or a robin on the wing,
But I feel so gay, in a melancholy way,
That it might as well be spring...
It might as well be spring.

It Never Entered My Mind

Words by Lorenz Hart
Music by Richard Rodgers

from *Higher and Higher*

I don't care if there's powder on my nose.
I don't care if my hairdo is in place.
I've lost the very meaning of repose.
I never put a mudpack on my face.
Oh who'd have thought
That I'd walk in a daze now?
I never go to shows at night,
But just to matinees now.
I see the show
And home I go.

Refrain 1:
Once I laughed when I heard you saying
That I'd be playing solitaire,
Uneasy in my easy chair,
It never entered my mind.
Once you told me I was mistaken,
That I'd awaken with the sun
And order orange juice for one.
It never entered my mind.
You have what I lack myself,
And now I even have to scratch my
    back myself.
Once you warned me that if
    you scorned me
I'd sing the maiden's prayer again
And wish that you were there again
To get into my hair again.
It never entered my mind.

Refrain 2:
Once you said in your funny lingo
I'd sit at bingo day and night
And never get the numbers right.
It never entered my mind.
Once you told me I'd stay up Sunday
To read the Monday-morning dirt
And find you're merging with some skirt.
It never entered my mind.
Life is not so sweet alone.

The man who came to dinner lets
    me eat alone.
I confess it, I didn't guess it,
That I would sit and mope again
And all the while I'd hope again.
It never entered my mind!

It Only Takes a Moment

Music and Lyric by Jerry Herman

from *Hello, Dolly!*

Cornelius:
It only takes a moment
For your eyes to meet and then,
Your heart knows, in a moment,
You will never be alone again.

I held her for an instant,
But my arms felt sure and strong.
It only takes a moment
To be loved a whole life long.

ADDITIONAL LYRICS
Spoken:
It only—
Chorus (Sung):
Takes a moment,
But his arms felt sure and strong.
It only takes a moment.

Mrs. Molloy:
He held me for an instant,
But his arms felt safe and strong.
It only takes a moment
To be loved a whole life long.

Cornelius:
And that is all
That love's about.
Mrs. Molloy:
And we'll recall,
When time runs out,
Both:
That it only took a moment,
To be loved a whole life long.

It's De-Lovely

Words and Music by Cole Porter

from *Red, Hot and Blue!*

He:
I feel a sudden urge to sing
The kind of ditty that invokes the spring,
So control your desire to curse
While I crucify the verse.
She:
This verse you've started seems to me
The Tin-Pantithesis of melody,
So spare me, please, the pain,
Just skip the damn thing and sing the refrain.
He:
Mi, mi, mi, mi,
Re, re, re, re,
Do, sol, mi do, la, si.
She:
Take it away.

Refrain:
The night is young, the skies are clear,
So if you want to go walking, dear,
It's delightful, it's delicious, it's de-lovely.
I understand the reason why
You're sentimental, 'cause so am I,
It's delightful, it's delicious, it's de-lovely.
You can tell at a glance
What a swell night this is for romance,
You can hear dear Mother Nature
    murmuring low,
"Let yourself go."

So please be sweet, chickadee,
And when I kiss you, just say to me,
"It's delightful, it's delicious,
It's delectable, it's delirious,
It's dilemma, it's delimit, it's deluxe,
It's de-lovely."

She:
Oh, charming sir the way you sing
Would break the heart of
    Missus Crosby's Bing,
For the tone of your tra la la
Has that certain je ne sais quoi.
He:
O, thank thee kindly, winsome wench,
But 'stead of falling into Berlitz French
Just warble to me, please,
The beautiful strain in plain Brooklynese.
She:
Mi, mi, mi, mi,
Re, re, re, re,
Do, sol, mi, do, la, si.
He:
Take it away.

Time marches on and soon it's plain
You've won my heart and I've lost my brain,
It's delightful, it's delicious, it's de-lovely.
Life seems so sweet that we decide
It's in the bag to get unified,
It's delightful, it's delicious, it's de-lovely.
See the crowd in that church,
See the proud parson plopped on his perch,
Set the sweet beat of that organ,
   sealing our doom,
"Here goes the groom, boom!"
How they cheer and how they smile
As we go galloping down the aisle.
"It's divine, dear, it's diveen, dear,
It's de-wunderbar, it's de victory,
It's de vallop, it's de vinner, it's de voika,
It's de-lovely.

The knot is tied and so we take
A few hours off to eat wedding cake,
It's delightful, it's delicious, it's de-lovely.
It feels so fine to be a bride,
And how's the groom? Why he's slightly fried,
It's delightful, it's delicious, it's de-lovely.
To the pop of champagne,
Off we hop in a plush little plane
Till a night light through the darkness
   cozily calls,
"Niagara Falls"
All's well, my love, our day's complete,
And what a beautiful bridal suite,
"It's de-reamy, it's de-rowsy,
It's de-reverie, it's de-rhapsody,
It's de-regal, it's de-royal, it's de-Ritz,
It's de-lovely.

We settle down as man and wife
To solve the riddle called "married life,"
It's delightful, it's delicious, it's de-lovely.
We're on the crest, we have no cares,
We're just a couple of honey bears,
It's delightful, it's delicious, it's de-lovely.
All's as right as right can be
Till, one night, at my window I see
An absurd bird with a bundle hung on his
   nose—
"Get baby clothes."
Those eyes of yours are filled with joy
When Nurse appears and cries, "It's a boy,
He's appalling, he's appealing
He's a pollywog, he's a paragon,
He's a Popeye, he's a panic, he's a pip,
He's de-lovely."

It's Today

Music and Lyric by Jerry Herman

from *Mame*

Light the candles,
Get the ice out,
Roll the rug up,
It's today!

Though it may not be anyone's birthday,
And though it's far from the first of the year,
I know that this very minute
Has history in it,
We're here!

It's a time for—
Makin' merry.
And so I'm for—
Makin' hay!
Tune the 'grand' up,
Dance your shoes off,
Strike the band up,
It's today!

And we're livin',
And we're well, gang,
So raise hell, gang,
While we may.
Call the cops out,
Raise a racket,
Pull the stops out,
Pull out the stops!
It's today!

Light the candles,
Fill the punchbowl,
Throw confetti,
It's today!

Life can also be lived on a weekday,
So don't depend on a holiday date,
If you need New Year's to bubble,
Then order a double and wait—
Doo doo doo doo doo,
Doo doo doo doo dah!

There's a thank you,
You can give life,
If you live life,
All the way.
Pour the scotch out,
Hold the roof down,
Fellas, watch out,
It's today!

It's a time for—
Makin' merry.
And so I'm for—
Makin' hay!
Tune the 'grand' up,
Call the cops out,
Strike the band up,
Pull the stops out,
Hallelujah!
It's today!
(Spoken) Hey!

June Is Bustin' Out All Over

Lyrics by Oscar Hammerstein II
Music by Richard Rodgers

from *Carousel*

March went out like a lion,
A-whippin' up the water in the bay.
Then April cried
And stepped aside,
And along come pretty little May!

May was full of promises,
But she didn't keep 'em quick enough
    fer some,
And a crowd of Doubtin' Thomases
Was predictin' that the summer'd
    never come.

But it's comin', by gum!
Y' ken feel it come,
Y' ken feel it in yer heart,
Y' ken see it in the ground,
Y' ken see it in the trees,
Y' ken hear it in the breeze—
Look around, look around, look around!

June is bustin' out all over!
All over the meadow and the hill,
Buds're bustin' outa bushes,
And the rompin' river pushes
Ev'ry little wheel that wheels beside a mill.
June is bustin' out all over!
The feelin' is gettin' so intense
That the young Virginia creepers
Hev been huggin' the bejeepers
Outa all the mornin' glories on the fence.
Because it's June!
June, June, June—
Jest because it's June—June—June!

Fresh and alive and gay and young,
June is a love song sweetly sung.

June is bustin' out all over!
The saplin's are bustin' out with sap!
Love hes found my brother, "Junior,"
And my sister's even lunier,
And my ma is gettin' kittenish with Pap.
June is bustin' out all over!
To ladies the men are payin' court.
Lotsa ships are kept at anchor
Jest because the captains hanker
Fer a comfort they ken only get in port!
Because it's June!
June, June, June—
Jest because it's June—June—June!

June makes the bay look bright and new,
Sails gleamin' white on sunlit blue.

June is bustin' out all over!
The ocean is full of Jacks and Jills.
With her little tail a-swishin'
Ev'ry lady fish is wishin'
That a male would come and grab her by
    the gills!
June is bustin' out all over!
The sheep aren't sleepin' any more.
All the rams that chase the ewe sheep
Are determined there'll be new sheep,
And the ewe sheep aren't even keepin' score!
On accounta it's June!
June, June, June—
Jest because it's June—June—June!

Just in Time

Words by Betty Comden and Adolph Green
Music by Jule Styne

from *Bells Are Ringing*

I was resting comfortably, face down in the gutter.
Life was serene, I knew where I was at.
"There's no hope for him,"
My dearest friends would mutter.
I was something dragged in by the cat.
Then…

Just in time,
I found you just in time.
Before you came
My time was running low.

I was lost,
The losing dice were tossed,
My bridges were all crossed,
Nowhere to go.

Now you're here
And now I know just where I'm going,
No more doubt or fear,
I've found my way.

For love came just in time.
You found me just in time,
And changed my lonely life,
That lovely day.

The Last Night of the World

Music by Claude-Michel Schönberg
Lyrics by Richard Maltby Jr. and Alain Boublil
Adapted from original French Lyrics by Alain Boublil

from *Miss Saigon*

Chris:

In a place that won't let us feel,
In a life where nothing seems real
I have found you,
I have found you.

Kim:

In a world that's moving too fast,
In a world where nothing can last,
I will hold you,
I will hold you.

Chris:

Our lives will change when tomorrow comes.
Kim:

Tonight our hearts dream the distant drums.
Chris:

And we have music alright tearing the night.
A song played on a solo saxophone.
A crazy sound, a lonely sound,
Both:

A cry that tells me love goes on and on.
Played on a solo saxophone,
It's telling me to hold you tight,
And dance like it's the last night of the world.

Chris:

On the other side of the earth,
There's a place where life still has worth.
I will take you.

Kim:

I'll go with you.
Chris:

You won't believe all the things you'll see.
I know 'cause you'll see them all with me.

Both:

If we're together, well then,
We'll hear it again,
A song played on a solo saxophone.
A crazy sound, a lonely sound.
A cry that tells us love goes on and on.
Played on a solo saxophone.
It's telling me to hold you tight
And dance like it's the last night of the world.

Kim:

Dreams were all I ever knew.
Chris:

Dreams you won't need when I'm through.
Both:

Anywhere we may be I will sing with you our
    song.
So stay with me and hold me tight
And dance like it's the last night of the world.

The Ladies Who Lunch

Music and Lyrics by Stephen Sondheim

from *Company*

Here's to the ladies who lunch—
Everybody laugh.
Lounging in their caftans and planning a
 brunch
On their own behalf.
Off to the gym
Then to a fitting
Claiming they're fat.
And looking grim
'Cause they've been sitting choosing a hat.

Spoken:
Does anyone still wear a hat?

I'll drink to that.

Here's to the girls who stay smart.
Aren't they a gas?
Rushing to their classes in optical art,
Wishing it would pass.
Another long, exhausting day,
Another thousand dollars.
A matinee:
A Pinter play,
Perhaps a piece of Mahler's.
I'll drink to that—
And one for Mahler.

Here's to the girls who play wife.
Aren't they too much?
Keeping house, but clutching a copy of
 Life—
Just to keep in touch.
The ones who follow the rules
And meet themselves at the schools—
Too busy to know that they're fools.
Aren't they a gem?
I'll drink to them!
Let's all drink to them!

Here's to the girls who just watch.
Aren't they the best?
When they get depressed,
 it's a bottle of Scotch—
Plus a little jest.
Another chance to disapprove,
Another brilliant zinger.
Another reason not to move,
Another vodka stinger.

Scream:
Aaah…

I'll drink to that.

So here's to the girls on the go,
Everybody tries.
Look into their eyes and you'll
   see what they know:
Everybody dies.
A toast to that invincible bunch,
The dinosaurs surviving the crunch,
Let's hear it for the ladies who lunch:
Everybody rise!
Rise! Rise!
Rise! Rise!
Rise! Rise!
Rise!

The Lady Is a Tramp

Words by Lorenz Hart
Music by Richard Rodgers

from *Babes in Arms*

I've wined and dined on Mulligan stew
And never wished for turkey
As I hitched and hiked and grifted too,
From Maine to Albuquerque.
Alas, I missed the Beaux Arts Ball,
And what is twice as sad,
I was never at a party
Where they honored Noël Ca'ad.
But social circles spin too fast for me.
My hobohemia is the place for me

I get too hungry for dinner at eight.
I like the theatre, but never come late.
I never bother with people I hate.
That's why the lady is a tramp.
I don't like crap games with barons
    and earls.
Won't go to Harlem in ermine
    and pearls.
Won't dish the dirt with the
    rest of the girls.
That's why the lady is a tramp.
I like the free, fresh wind in my hair,
Life without care.
I'm broke—it's oke.
Hate California—it's cold and damp.
That's why the lady is a tramp.

I go to Coney—the beach is divine.
I go to ball games—the bleachers are fine.
I follow Winchell and read every line.
That's why the lady is a tramp.
I like a prizefight that isn't a fake.
I love the rowing on Central Park Lake.
I go to operas and stay wide awake.
That's why the lady is a tramp.
I like the green grass under my shoes.
What can I lose?
I'm flat! That's that!
I'm all alone when I lower my lamp.
That's why the lady is a tramp.

Don't know the reason for cocktails at five.
I don't like flying—I'm glad I'm alive.
I crave affection, but not when I drive.
That's why the lady is a tramp.
Folks go to London and leave me behind.
I missed the crowning, Queen Mary won't
    mind.
I don't play Scarlett in Gone with the Wind.
That's why the lady is a tramp.
I like to hang my hat where I please.
Sail with the breeze.
No dough—heigh-ho!
I love La Guardia and think he's a champ.
That's why the lady is a tramp.

Girls get massages, they cry and they moan.
Tell Lizzie Arden to leave me alone.
I'm not too hot, but my shape is my own.
That's why the lady is a tramp!
The food at Sardi's is perfect, no doubt.
I wouldn't know what the Ritz is about.
I drop a nickel and coffee comes out.
That's why the lady is a tramp!
I like the sweet, fresh rain in my face.
Diamonds and lace,
No got—so what?
For Robert Taylor I whistle and stamp.
That's why the lady is a tramp!

Let's Have Another Cup o' Coffee

Words and Music by Irving Berlin

from the Stage Production *Face the Music*

Why worry when skies are gray?
Why should we complain?
Let's laugh at the cloudy day.
Let's sing in the rain.
Song writers say the storm quickly passes.
That's their philosophy.
They see the world through rose-colored glasses.
Why shouldn't we?

Just around the corner,
There's a rainbow in the sky.
So let's have another cup o' coffee,
And let's have another piece o' pie!

Trouble's just a bubble,
And the clouds will soon roll by.
So let's have another cup o' coffee,
And let's have another piece o' pie!

Let a smile be your umbrella,
For it's just an April show'r.
Even John D. Rockefeller
Is looking for the silver lining.

Mister Herbert Hoover
Says that now's the time to buy.
So let's have another cup o' coffee,
And let's have another piece o' pie!

Let's Take an Old-Fashioned Walk

Words and Music by Irving Berlin

from the Stage Production *Miss Liberty*

Some couples go for a buggy ride
When they start caring a lot.
Others will bicycle side by side,
Out to some romantic spot.
But when you haven't a sou,
There's only one thing to do.

Refrain:
Let's take an old-fashioned walk.
I'm just bursting with talk.
What a tale could be told,
If we went for an old-fashioned walk.
Let's take a stroll through the park.
Down a lane where it's dark,
And a heart that's controlled
May relax on an old-fashioned walk.
I know for a couple
Who seem to be miles apart,
There's nothing like walking,
And having a "heart to heart."
I know a girl who declined.
Couldn't make up her mind.
She was wrapped up and sold
Coming home from an old-fashioned walk.

I used to dream of a millionaire,
Handsome and rich from the States.
Taking me out for a breath of air,
Saying, "The carriage awaits."
But since you haven't a sou,
And I have nothing to do:

Refrain

Let's Not Talk About Love

Words and Music by Cole Porter

from *Let's Face It*

Relax for one moment, my Jerry,
Come out of your dark monastery,
While Venus is beaming above,
Darling, let's talk about love.

My buddies all tell me selectees
Are expected by ladies to neck-tease,
I could talk about love and why not?
But believe me, it wouldn't be so hot.

So let's talk about frogs,
Let's talk about toads,
Let's try to solve the riddle
Why chickens cross roads,
Let's talk about games,
Let's talk about sports,
Let's have a big debate about
Ladies in shorts.
Let's check on the veracity
Of Barrymore's bibacity,
And why his drink capacity
Should get so much publicity,
Let's even have a huddle over
Ha'vard Univasity,
But let's not talk about love.

Let's wish him good luck,
Let's wish him more pow'r
That Fiorella fella,
My favorite flow'r,
Let's curse the Old Guard
And Hamilton Fish,
Forgive me, dear,

If Fish is your favorite dish,
Let's write a tune that's playable,
A ditty swing-and-swayable,
Or say whatever's sayable
About the Tow'r of Ba-a-bel,
Let's cheer for the career of
Itty-bitty Betty Gra-a-ble,
But let's not talk about love.

Let's talk about drugs,
Let's talk about dope,
Let's try to picture Paramount,
Minus Bob Hope.
Let's start a new dance,
Let's try a new step,
Or investigate the cause
Of Missus Roosevelt's pep,
Why not discuss, my dee-a-rie,
The life of Wallace Bee-a-ry,
Or bring a jeroboam on
And write a drunken poem on
Timidity, stupidity,
Solidity, frigidity,
Avidity, turbidity,
Manhattan and viscidity,
Fatality, morality,
Legality, finality,
Neutrality, reality
Or Southern hospitality,
Pomposity, verbosity,
I'm losing my velocity,
But let's not talk about love.

ADDITIONAL LYRICS
Refrain 2:
So let's talk about frogs,
Let's talk about toads,
Let's try to solve the riddle
Why chickens cross roads,
Let's talk about games,
Let's talk about sports,
Let's have a big debate about
Ladies in shorts.
Let's question the synonymy
Of freedom and autonomy,
Let's delve into astronomy,
Political economy,
Or if you're feeling biblical,
The book of Deuteronomy,
But let's not talk about love.

Let's ride the New Deal,
Like Senator Glass,
Let's telephone to Ickes
And order more gas,
Let's curse the Old Guard
And Hamilton Fish,
Forgive me, dear,
If Fish is your favorite dish.
Let's heap some hot profanities
On Hitler's inhumanities,
Let's argue if insanity's
The cause of his inanities,
Let's weigh the Shubert Follies
With The Ear-rl Carroll Vanities,
But let's not talk about love.

Let's talk about drugs,
Let's talk about dope,
Let's try to picture Paramount
Minus Bob Hope,
Let's start a new dance,
Let's try a new step,
Or investigate the cause
Of Missus Roosevelt's pep,
Why not discus, my dee-a-rie,
The life of Wallace Bee-a-ry,
Or bring a jeroboam on
And write a drunken poem on
Astrology, mythology,
Geology, philology,
Pathology, psychology,
Electro-physiology,
Spermology, phrenology,
I owe you an apology,
But let's not talk about love.

(continues)

("Let's Not Talk About Love," *continued*)

Refrain 3:
Let's speak of Lamarr,
The Hedy so fair,
Why does she let Joan Bennett
Wear all her old hair?
If you know Garbo,
Then tell me this news,
Is it a fact the Navy's launched
All her old shoes?
Let's check on the veracity
Of Barrymore's bibacity,
And why his drink capacity
Should get so much publicity,
Let's even have a huddle over
Ha'vard Univassity,
But let's not talk about love.

Let's wish him good luck,
Let's wish him more pow'r,
That Fiorella fella,
My favorite flow'r,
Let's get some champagne
From over the seas,
And drink to Sammy Goldwyn,
Include me out please.
Let's write a tune that's playable,
A ditty swing-and-swayable,
Or say whatever's sayable,
About the Tow'r of Ba-a-bel,
Let's cheer for the career of
Itty-bitty Betty Gra-a-bel,
But let's not talk about love.

In case you play cards,
I've got some right here,
So how about a game
O' gin-rummy, my dear?
Or if you feel warm
And bathin's your whim,
Let's get in the all-together
And enjoy a short swim,
No honey, Ah suspect you all
Of bein' intellectual,
And so, instead of gushin' on,
Let's have a big discussion on
Timidity, stupidity,
Solidity, frigidity,
Avidity, turbidity,
Manhattan, and viscidity,
Fatality, morality,
Legality, finality,
Neutrality, reality,
Or Southern hospitality,
Pomposity, verbosity,
You're losing your velocity
But let's not talk about love.

A Little Rumba Numba

Words and Music by Cole Porter

from *Let's Face It*

A little rumba numba,
Down Argentina way,
Made me forget to slumba,
As through a dance she'd sway,

Singing, "Hear the stars above,"
Singing, "Ay-ay-ay, Ay-ay-ay,
Ay-ay-ay, Ay-ay-ay."

That little rumba numba,
Is now my darling wife,
"Ay-ay-ay…"

That little rumba numba
And I fell so in love,
That while the world would slumba,
We'd—And though we never slumba,
We lead a lovely life,
Singing, "Ay-ay-ay…"

A Little More Mascara

Music and Lyric by Jerry Herman

from *La Cage Aux Folles*

Once again, I'm a little depressed
By the tired old face that I see,
Once again, it is time to be someone
Who's anyone other than me.
With a rare combination of
    girlish excitement
And manly restraint,
I position my precious assortment
    of powders
And pencils and paint.
So, whenever I feel that my place
    in this world
Is beginning to crash,
I apply one great stroke of mascara
    to my
Rather limp upper lash.
And I can cope again,
Good God!
There's hope again.

When life is a real bitch again,
And my old sense of humor has up and
    gone,
It's time for the big switch again,
I put a little more mascara on.

When I count my crow's feet again,
And tire of this perpetual marathon,
I put down the john seat again,
And put a little more mascara on.

And ev'rything's sparkle dust,
Bugle beads,
Ostrich plumes,
When it's a beaded lash—
That you look—
Through.
'Cause when I feel glamorous,
Elegant,
Beautiful,
The world that I'm looking at's
Beautiful,
Too!

When my little road has a few bumps again,
And I need something level to lean upon,
I put on my sling pumps again,
And wham! This ugly duckling is a swan!
So when my spirit starts to sag,
I hustle out my highest drag,
And put a little more mascara on.

And ev'rything's ankle straps,
Maribu,
Shalimar!
It's worth sucking in my gut,
And gird'ling
My rear.
'Cause ev'rything's ravishing,
Sensual,
Fabulous,
When Albin is tucked away,
And Zaza
Is here!

When ev'rything slides down the old tubes again,
And my old self-esteem has begun to drift,
I strap on my fake boobs again,
And literally give myself a lift!
So when it's cold and when it's bleak,
I simply rouge the other cheek,
For I can face another day
In slipper satin lingerie,
To make depression disappear,
I screw some rhinestones on my ear,
And put my broaches and tiara
And a little more mascara on!

A Little Skipper from Heaven Above

Words and Music by Cole Porter

from *Red, Hot and Blue!*

The raging Sou'wester was over,
It was calm and the heavens had cleared,
The sails were gently flapping,
The sailors all a-napping,
When their hero, Captain Cosgrove, appeared.

It was obvious he had been crying,
And he seemed to have lost all his poise.
As he stood there, so stark,
And was heard to remark,
"I've got something to say to you boys."

I'm about to become a mother,
I'm only a girl, not a boy.
Years ago, I disguised as my brother,
And went rolling down to Rio,
Ship ahoy!

Though it hurts me to leave you, m' hearties,
Still you must understand, it was love,
And I'm about to give birth
To the sweetest thing on earth,
A little skipper from heaven above.

Look to the Rainbow

Words by E.Y. Harburg
Music by Burton Lane

from *Finian's Rainbow*

On the day I was born,
Said my father, said he,
I've an elegant legacy
Waitin' for ye.
'Tis a rhyme for your lip
And a song for your heart,
To sing it whenever
The world falls apart.

Refrain:
Look, look, look to the rainbow,
Follow it over the hill and stream.
Look, look, look to the rainbow,
Follow the fellow who follows a dream.

So I bundled me heart,
And I roamed the world free,
To the east with the lark,
To the west with the sea.
And I search'd all the earth,
And I scann'd all the skies.
But I found it at last
In my own true love's eyes.

Refrain

Follow the fellow,
Follow the fellow,
Follow the fellow who follows a dream.

Lost in the Stars

Words by Maxwell Anderson
Music by Kurt Weill

from the Musical Production *Lost in the Stars*

Before Lord God made the sea and the land,
He held all the stars in the palm of His hand,
And they ran through his fingers like grains of sand,
And one little star fell alone.

Then the Lord God hunted through the wide night air
For the little dark star on the wind down there
And he started and promised he'd take special care
So it wouldn't get lost again.

Now a man don't mind if the stars grow dim
And the clouds blow over and darken him,
So long as the Lord God's watching over them,
Keeping track how it all goes on.

But I've been walking through the night and day
Till my eyes get weary and my head turns gray,
And sometimes it seems maybe God's gone away,
Forgetting the promise that we heard him say
And we're lost out here in the stars.

Little stars, big stars, blowing through the night,
And we're lost out here in the stars,
Little stars, big stars, blowing through the night,
And we're lost out here in the stars.

Love Changes Everything

Music by Andrew Lloyd Webber
Lyrics by Don Black and Charles Hart

from *Aspects of Love*

Love, love changes everything,
Hands and faces, earth and sky.
Love, love changes everything,
How you live and how you die.

Love can make the summer fly,
Or a night seem like a lifetime.

Yes love, love changes everything,
Now I tremble at your name.
Nothing in the world
Will ever be the same.

Love, love changes everything,
Days are longer, words mean more.
Love, love changes everything,
Pain is deeper than before.

Love will turn your world around,
And that world will last forever.

Yes love, love changes everything,
Brings you glory, brings you shame.
Nothing in the world
Will ever be the same.

Off into the world we go,
Planning futures, shaping years.
Love bursts in, and suddenly,
All our wisdom disappears.

Love makes fools of everyone,
All the rules we make are broken.

Yes love, love changes everyone.
Live or perish in its flame.
Love will never, never let you
Be the same.
Love will never, never let you
Be the same.

Love, Look Away

Lyrics by Oscar Hammerstein II
Music by Richard Rodgers

from *Flower Drum Song*

Love, look away!
Love, look away from me.
Fly when you pass my door,
Fly and get lost at sea.

Call it a day.
Love, let us say we're through.
No good are you for me.
No good am I for you.
Wanting you so, I try too much.
After you go, I cry too much.

Love, look away.
Lonely though I may be,
Leave me and set me free,
Look away, look away, look away from me.

Lover, Come Back to Me

Lyrics by Oscar Hammerstein II
Music by Sigmund Romberg

from *The New Moon*

You went away, I let you,
We broke the ties that bind;
I wanted to forget you
And leave the past behind.
Still, the magic of the night I met you
Seems to stay forever in my mind.

The sky was blue
And high above
The moon was new
And so was love.
This eager heart of mine was singing:
"Lover, where can you be?"

You came at last,
Love had its day,
That day is past,
You've gone away.
This aching heart of mine is singing:
"Lover, come back to me!"

When I remember every little thing you used to do,
I'm so lonely,
Every road I walk along I've walked along with you,
No wonder I am lonely.

The sky is blue,
The night is cold,
The moon is new,
But love is old,
And, while I'm waiting here,
This heart of mine is singing:
"Lover, come back to me!"

Mad About the Boy

Words and Music by Noel Coward

from *Words and Music*

I met him at a party just a couple of
  years ago,
He was rather over hearty and ridiculous,
But as I'd seen him on the screen,
He cast a certain spell.

I bask'd in his attraction for a couple of
  hours or so,
His manners were a fraction
  too meticulous.
If he was real or not I couldn't tell,
But like a silly fool I fell.

Mad about the boy,
I know it's stupid to be mad about the boy,
I'm so ashamed of it,
But must admit
The sleepless nights I've had about the boy.

On the silver screen,
He melts my foolish heart in ev'ry
  single scene,
Although I'm quite aware
That here and there
Are traces of the cad about the boy.

Lord knows I'm not a fool girl,
I really shouldn't care.
Lord knows I'm not a school girl,
In the flurry of her first affair.

Will it every cloy?
This odd diversity of misery and joy,
I'm feeling quite insane
And young again,
And all because I'm mad about the boy.

It seems a little silly
For a girl of my age and weight
To walk down Piccadilly
In a haze of love,
It ought to take a good deal more
To get a bad girl down.

I should have been exempt,
For my particular kind of fate
Has taught me such contempt
For ev'ry phase of love,
And now I've been and spent
My last half-crown,
To weep about a painted clown.

Mad about the boy,
It's pretty funny, but I'm mad about the boy.
He has a gay appeal
That makes me feel
There's maybe something sad about the boy.

Walking down the street,
His eyes look out at me from people
   that I meet,
I can't believe it's true,
But when I'm blue,
In some strange way I'm glad about the boy.

I'm hardly sentimental,
Love isn't so sublime,
I have to pay my rental
And I can't afford to waste much time.

If I could employ
A little magic that would finally destroy
This dream that pains me
And enchains me,
But I can't, because I'm mad about the boy.

Many Moons Ago

Music by Mary Rodgers
Words by Marshall Barer

from *Once Upon a Mattress*

Many moons ago,
In a far-off place,
Lived a handsome prince
With a gloomy face,
For he did not have a bride.

Oh, he sighed "alas,"
And he pined alas,
But alas, the prince
Couldn't find a lass
Who would suit his mother's pride.

Refrain:
For a princess is a delicate thing,
Delicate and dainty as a dragonfly's wing.
You can recognize a lady by her elegant air,
But a genuine princess is exceedingly rare.

On a stormy night,
To the castle door,
Came the lass the prince
Had been waiting for.
"I'm a princess lost," quoth she.

But the queen was cool
And remained aloof,
And she said: "Perhaps,"
But she'll need some proof.
"I'll prepare a test and see."

Spoken:
"I will test her thus,"
The old queen said:
"I'll put twenty downy mattresses
Upon her bed,
And between those twenty mattresses
I'll place a tiny pea.
If that pea disturbs her slumber,
Then a true princess is she."

Sung:
Now, the bed was soft
And extremely tall,
But the dainty lass
Didn't sleep at all.
And she told them so next day.

Said the queen, "My dear,
If you felt that pea,
Then we've proof enough
Of your royalty.
Let the wedding music play."
Spoken:
And the people shouted quietly:
"Hooray."

Refrain

Marian the Librarian

By Meredith Willson

from Meredith Willson's *The Music Man*

Marian,
Madam librarian.

What can I do, my dear,
To catch your ear?
I love you madly, madly,
Madam librarian, Marian.
Heaven help us,
If the library caught on fire,
And the volunteer hose brigade men
Had to whisper the news to Marian,
Madam librarian.

What can I say, my dear,
To make it clear?
I need you badly, badly,
Madam librarian, Marian.
If I stumbled,
And I busted my what-you-ma-call-it,
I could lie on your floor unnoticed,
'Til my body had turned to carrion,
Madam librarian.

Now in the moonlight,
A man could sing it,
In the moonlight.
And a fellow would know that his darling
Had heard ev'ry word of his song,
With the moonlight
Helping along.

But when I try, in here,
To tell you, dear,
I love you madly, madly,
Madam librarian, Marian,
It's a long lost cause I can never win,
For the civilized world accepts
As unforgivable sin
Any talking out loud with any librarian,
Such as Marian,
Madam librarian.

Me and My Girl

Words by Douglas Furber and Arthur Rose
Music by Noel Gay

from *Me and My Girl*

Life's an empty thing,
Life can be so awful lonesome,
If you're always on your own some,
Life's an empty thing.

Life's a diff'rent thing,
When you've found your one and only,
Then you feel no longer lonely,
Life's a happy thing.

Ev'rything was topsy-turvy,
Life seemed all wrong,
But it came all right
As soon as you came along.

Me and my girl,
Meant for each other,
Sent for each other,
And liking it so.
Me and my girl,
'Sno use pretending,
We knew the ending
A long time ago.

Some little clown,
With a big steeple,
Just a few people
That both of us know.
And we'll have love,
Laughter,
Be happy ever after,
Me and my girl.

Mein Herr

Words by Fred Ebb
Music by John Kander

from the Musical *Cabaret*

You have to understand the way I am,
  mein Herr.
A tiger is a tiger, not a lamb, mein Herr.
You'll never turn the vinegar to jam,
  mein Herr.
So I do what I do.
When I'm through, then I'm through,
And I'm through. Toodle-oo!

Refrain 1:
Bye bye, mein lieber Herr,
Farewell mein lieber Herr,
It was a fine affair,
But now it's over.
And though I used to care,
I need the open air,
You're better off without me,
Mein Herr.

Refrain 2:
Don't dab your eye, mein Herr,
Or wonder why, mein Herr,
I've always said that I
Was a rover.
You musn't knit your brow.
You should have known by now
You'd ev'ry cause to doubt me,
Mein Herr.

The continent of Europe is so wide,
  mein Herr.
Not only up and down, but side to side,
  mein Herr.
I couldn't ever cross it if I tried, mein Herr.
But I do what I can,
Inch by inch, step by step,
Mile by mile, man by man.

Refrain 1

Refrain 2

Bye bye mein lieber Herr,
Auf wiedersehen, mein Herr.
Es war sehr gut, mein Herr,
Und vorbei.
Du kennst mich wohl, mein Herr,
Ach, lebe wohl, mein Herr.
Du sollst mich nie mehr sehen,
Mein Herr.

Refrain 1

You'll get on without me,
Mein Herr.

Memory

Music by Andrew Lloyd Webber
Text by Trevor Nunn after T.S. Eliot

from *Cats*

Midnight.
Not a sound from the pavement.
Has the moon lost her memory?
She is smiling alone.
In the lamp-light
The withered leaves collect at my feet
And the wind
Begins to moan.

Memory.
All alone in the moonlight
I can smile at the old days,
I was beautiful then.
I remember
The time I knew what happiness was,
Let the memory
Live again.

Ev'ry street lamp seems to beat
A fatalistic warning.
Someone mutters
And a street lamp gutters
And soon it will be morning.

Daylight.
I must wait for the sunrise.
I must think of a new life
And I mustn't give in.
When the dawn comes
Tonight will be a memory too
And a new day
Will begin.

Burnt out ends of smoky days
The stale cold smell of the morning;
The street lamp dies
Another night is over,
Another day is dawning.

Touch me.
It's so easy to leave me
All alone with the memory
Of my days in the sun.
If you touch me
You'll understand what happiness is.
Look, a new day
Has begun.

Mister Snow

Lyrics by Oscar Hammerstein II
Music by Richard Rodgers

from *Carousel*

His name is Mister Snow,
And an upstandin' man is he.
He comes home ev'ry night in his
   round-bottomed boat,
With a net full of herring from the sea.

An almost perfect beau,
As refined as a girl could wish,
But he spends so much time in his
   round-bottomed boat,
That he can't seem to lose the smell of fish!

The fust time he kissed me,
   the whiff of his clo'es
Knocked me flat on the floor of the room,
But now that I love him,
   my heart's in my nose,
And fish is my fav'rite perfume!

Last night he spoke quite low,
And a fair spoken man is he,
And he said, "Miss Pipperidge, I'd like it fine
If I could be wed with a wife,
And, indeed, Miss Pipperidge,
   if you'll be mine,
I'll be yours fer the rest of my life!"

Next moment we were promised!
And now my mind's in a maze,
Fer all it ken do is look forward to
That wonderful day of days.

When I marry Mister Snow,
The flowers'll be buzzin' with the
   hum of bees,
The birds'll make a racket in the
   churchyard trees,
When I marry Mister Snow.

Then it's off to home we'll go,
And both of us'll look a little dreamy-eyed,
A-drivin' to a cottage by the ocean side,
Where the salty breezes blow.

He'll carry me 'cross the threshold,
And I'll be as meek as a lamb.
Then he'll set me on my feet,
And I'll say, kinda sweet,
Spoken:
"Well, Mister Snow, here I am!"

Then I'll kiss him so he'll know
That ev'rythin' 'll be as right as right ken be,
A-livin' in a cottage by the sea with me,
For I love that Mister Snow,
That young, seafarin', bold and darin',
Big, bewhiskered, over bearin' darlin',
Mister Snow!

Mr. Wonderful

Words and Music by Jerry Bock, Larry Holofcener and George David Weiss

from the Musical *Mr. Wonderful*

Why this feeling?
Why this glow?
Why the thrill when you say, "Hello!"?
It's a strange and tender magic you do.
Mr. Wonderful,
That's you!

Why this trembling when you speak?
Why this joy when you touch my cheek?
I must tell you what my heart knows is true:
Mr. Wonderful, that's you!

And why this longing to know your charms;
To spend forever here in your arms!
Oh! there's much more I could say,
But the words keep slipping away;
And I'm left with only one point of view:
Mr. Wonderful,
That's you!

One more thing, then I'm through;
Mr. Wonderful,
Mr. Wonderful,
Mr. Wonderful, I love you!

Mood Indigo

Words and Music by Duke Ellington, Irving Mills and Albany Bigard

from *Sophisticated Ladies*

You ain't been blue,
No, no, no.
You ain't been blue,
'Til you've had that Mood Indigo.
That feeling goes stealin' down to my shoes,
While I sit and sigh:
"Go 'long, blues."

Refrain:
Always get that mood indigo,
Since my baby said goodbye.
In the evenin' when lights are low,
I'm so lonesome I could cry,
'Cause there's nobody who cares about me,
I'm just a soul who's bluer than blue can be.
When I get that mood indigo,
I could lay me down and die.

Refrain

More I Cannot Wish You

By Frank Loesser

from *Guys and Dolls*

Velvet I can wish you,
For the collar of your coat,
And fortune smiling all along your way.

Refrain:
But more I cannot wish you,
Than to wish you find your love,
Your own true love, this day.

Mansions I can wish you,
Seven footmen all in red,
And calling cards upon a silver tray.

Refrain

Standing there,
Gazing at you,
Full of the bloom of youth.
Standing there,
Gazing at you,
With the sheep's eye,
And the lickerish tooth.

Music I can wish you,
Merry music, while you're young,
And wisdom,
When your hair has turned to gray.

Refrain

With sheep's eye,
And the lickerish tooth,
And the strong arms to carry you away.

© 1949, 1950 (Renewed) FRANK MUSIC CORP.

More Than You Know

Words by William Rose and Edward Eliscu
Music by Vincent Youmans

from *Great Day!*

Whether you are here or yonder,
Whether you are false or true,
Whether you remain or wander
I'm growing fonder of you.

Even though your friends forsake you,
Even though you don't succeed,
Wouldn't I be glad to take you,
Give you the break you need.

More than you know,
More than you know,
Man o' my heart, I love you so.
Lately I find you're on my mind,
More than you know.

Whether you're right,
Whether you're wrong,
Man o' my heart I'll string along.
You need me so
More than you'll ever know.

Loving you the way that I do
There's nothing I can do about it,
Loving may be all you can give
But honey, I can't live without it.

Oh, how I'd cry,
Oh, how I'd cry,
If you got tired and said, "Goodbye,"
More than I'd show
More than you'd ever know.

The Most Beautiful Girl in the World

Words by Lorenz Hart
Music by Richard Rodgers

from *Jumbo*

We used to spend the spring together
Before we learned to walk;
We used to laugh and sing together
Before we learned how to talk.
With no reason for the season,
Spring would end as it would start.
Now the season has a reason
And there's springtime in my heart.

Refrain:
The most beautiful girl in the world
Picks my ties out,
Eats my candy,
Drinks my brandy—
The most beautiful girl in the world.
The most beautiful girl in the world
Isn't Garbo, isn't Dietrich,
But the sweet trick
Who can make me believe it's a beautiful world.
Social, not a bit,
Natural kind of wit.
She'd shine anywhere,
And she hasn't got platinum hair.
The most beautiful house in the world
Has a mortgage—
What do I care?
It's goodbye care
When my slippers are next to the ones that belong
To the one and only beautiful girl in the world.

Much More

Words by Tom Jones
Music by Harvey Schmidt

from *The Fantasticks*

I'd like to swim in a clear blue stream
Where the water is icy cold,
Then go to town in a golden gown,
And have my fortune told.

Just once!
Just once!
Just once before I'm old!

I'd like to be not evil,
But a little worldly wise.
To be the kind of girl designed
To be kissed upon the eyes.

I'd like to dance till two o'clock
Or sometimes dance till dawn,
Or if the band could stand it,
Just go on, and on, and on!

Just once!
Just once!
Before the chance is gone!

I'd like to waste a week or two,
And never do a chore.
To wear my hair unfastened,
So it billows to the floor.

To do the things I've dreamed about,
But never done before.
Perhaps I'm bad, or wild, or mad,
With lots of grief in store,
But I want much more than keeping house!
Much more! Much more! Much more!

The Music of the Night

Music by Andrew Lloyd Webber
Lyrics by Charles Hart
Additional Lyrics by Richard Stilgoe

from *The Phantom of the Opera*

Night-time sharpens, heightens each sensation;
Darkness stirs and wakes imagination.
Silently the senses abandon their defenses.
Slowly, gently night unfurls its splendor;
Grasp it, sense it, tremulous and tender.
Turn your face away from the garish light of day,
Turn your thoughts away from cold unfeeling light
And listen to the music of the night.

Close your eyes and surrender to your darkest dreams!
Purge your thoughts of the life you knew before!
Close your eyes, let your spirit start to soar,
And you'll live as you've never lived before.

Softly, deftly, music shall caress you.
Hear it, feel it secretly possess you.
Open up your mind, let your fantasies unwind
In this darkness which you know you cannot fight,
The darkness of the music of the night.

Let your mind start a journey through a strange, new world;
Leave all thoughts of the world you knew before.
Let your soul take you where you long to be!
Only then can you belong to me.

Floating, falling, sweet intoxication.
Touch me, trust me, savour each sensation.
Let the dream begin, let your darker side give in
To the power of the music that I write,
The power of the music of the night.

You alone can make my song take flight,
Help me make the music of the night.

The Music That Makes Me Dance

Words by Bob Merrill
Music by Jule Styne

from *Funny Girl*

I add two and two,
The most simple addition,
Then swear that the figures are lying.
I'm a much better comic
Than mathematician,
'Cause I'm better on stage
Than at intermission.
And as far as the man is concerned,
If I've been burned,
I haven't learned.

I know he's around
When the sky and ground start in ringing.
I know when he's near
By the thunder I hear in advance.
His words and his words alone
Are the words that can start my heart singing.
And his is the only music that makes me dance.

He'll sleep and he'll rise
In the light of two eyes that adore him.
Bore him it might,
But he won't leave my sight for a glance.
In ev'ry way, ev'ry day,
I need less of myself and need more him—more him.
'Cause his is the only music that makes me dance.

My Heart Belongs to Daddy

Words and Music by Cole Porter

from *Leave It to Me!*

I used to fall
In love with all
Those boys who maul
Refined ladies.
But now I tell
Each young gazelle
To go to hell—
I mean, Hades.
For since I've come to care
For such a sweet millionaire.

Refrain 1:
While tearing off
A game of golf
I may make a play for the caddy.
But when I do,
I don't follow through
'Cause my heart belongs to Daddy.
If I invite
A boy, some night,
To dine on my fine finnan haddie,
I just adore
His asking for more,
But my heart belongs to Daddy.
Yes, my heart belongs to Daddy,
So I simply couldn't be bad.
Yes, my heart belongs to Daddy,
Da-da, da-da-da, da-da-da, dad!
So I want to warn you, laddie,
Tho' I know you're perfectly swell,
That my heart belongs to Daddy
'Cause my Daddy, he treats it so well.

Refrain 2:
Saint Patrick's Day,
Although I may
Be seen wearing green with a paddy,
I'm always sharp
When playing the harp,
'Cause my heart belongs to Daddy.
Though other dames
At football games
May long for a strong undergraddy,
I never dream
Of making the team
'Cause my heart belongs to Daddy.
Yes, my heart belongs to Daddy.
So I simply couldn't be bad.
Yes, my heart belongs to Daddy,
Da-da, da-da-da, da-da-da, dad!
So I want to warn you laddie,

Tho' I simply hate to be frank,
That I can't be mean to Daddy
'Cause my Da-da-da-daddy might spank.
In matters artistic
He's not modernistic
So Da-da-da-daddy might speak.

My Heart Stood Still

Words by Lorenz Hart
Music by Richard Rodgers

from *A Connecticut Yankee*

Note: These are the original show lyrics.

Martin:
I laughed at sweethearts
I met at schools;
All indiscreet hearts
Seemed romantic fools.
A house in Iceland
Was my heart's domain.
I saw your eyes;
Now castles rise in Spain!

Refrain:
I took one look at you,
That's all I meant to do,
And then my heart stood still!
My feet could step and walk,
My lips could move and talk,
And yet my heart stood still!
Though not a single word was spoken,
I could tell you knew,
That unfelt clasp of hands
Told me so well you knew.
I never lived at all
Until the thrill
Of that moment when
My heart stood still.

Sandy:
Through all my schooldays
I hated boys;
Those April Fool days
Brought me love-less joys.
I read my Plato,
Love I thought a sin;
But since your kiss,
I'm reading Missus Glynn!

Refrain

My Husband Makes Movies

Words and Music by Maury Yeston

from *Nine*

My husband makes movies.
To make them, he lives a kind of dream,
In which his actions aren't always
   what they seem.
He may be on to some unique
   romantic theme.

Some men catch fish,
Some men tie flies,
Some earn their living baking bread.
My husband, he goes a little crazy,
Making movies instead.

My husband spins fantasies.
He lives them, then gives them to you all.
While he was working on the film on
   ancient Rome,
He made the slave girls take the
   gladiators home.

Some men buy stocks,
Some men punch clocks,
Some leap where others fear to tread.
My husband, as author and director,
Makes up stories in his head.

Guido Contini, Luisa Contini,
Number one genius and number one fan.
Guido Contini, Luisa Contini,
Daughter of well-to-do Florentine clan,
Long ago, twenty years ago.

Once the names were,
Guido Contini, Luisa Del Forno,
Actress with dreams and a life of her own.
Passionate, wild, and in love with Livorno,
Singing with Guido all night on the phone,
Long ago, someone else ago.
How he needs me so,
And he'll be the last to know it.

My husband makes movies,
To make them, he makes himself obsessed.
He works for weeks on end,
   without a bit of rest,
No other way can he achieve his level best.

Some men read books,
Some shine their shoes,
Some retire early,
When they've seen the evening news.
My husband only rarely comes to bed,
My husband makes movies instead.
My husband makes movies.

My Romance

Words by Lorenz Hart
Music by Richard Rodgers

from *Jumbo*

I won't kiss your hand, madam,
Crazy for you though I am.
I'll never woo you on bended knee,
No, madam, not me.
We don't need that flowery fuss.
No sir, madam, not for us.

My romance
Doesn't have to have a moon in the sky.
My romance
Doesn't need a blue lagoon standing by.
No month of May,
No twinkling stars.
No hideaway,
No soft guitars.
My romance
Doesn't need a castle rising in Spain,
Nor a dance
To a constantly surprising refrain.
Wide awake,
I can make my most fantastic dreams come true.
My romance
Doesn't need a thing but you.

My Ship

Words by Ira Gershwin
Music by Kurt Weill

from the Musical Production *Lady in the Dark*

My ship has sails that are made of silk,
The decks are trimmed with gold.
And of jam and spice
There's a paradise
In the hold.

My ship's aglow with a million pearls
And rubies fill each bin.
The sun sits high
In a sapphire sky
When my ship comes in.

I can wait the years
'Til it appears
One fine day one spring,
But the pearls and such
They won't mean much
If there's missing just one thing.

I do not care if that day arrives,
That dream need never be,
If the ship I sing
Doesn't also bring
My own true love to me.

If the ship I sing
Doesn't also bring
My own true love to me.

N.Y.C.

Lyric by Martin Charnin
Music by Charles Strouse

from the Musical Production *Annie*

N.Y.C.,
What is it about you?
You're big, you're loud, you're tough.
N.Y.C.,
I go years without you,
Then I can't get enough.

Enough of cab drivers answering back,
In language far from pure,
Enough of frankfurters answering back,
Brother you know you're in:

N.Y.C.,
Too busy, too crazy.
Too hot,
Too cold;
Too late,
I'm sold,
Again,
On N.Y.C.

N.Y.C.,
The Hudson at sundown,
The roofs that scrape the sky.
N.Y.C.,
The rich and the rundown,
The big parade goes by.

Now, Frisco does have an int'resting bay,
Kansas City has good steaks,
Chicago's loop may be fun for a day,
New Orleans really shakes, but,

N.Y.C.,
You make 'em all postcards.
You snap,
You fizz.
The best
There is,
Is you,
Is N.Y.C.

Never Never Land

Lyric by Betty Comden and Adolph Green
Music by Jule Styne

from *Peter Pan*

I know a place where dreams are born,
And time is never planned.
It's not on any chart,
You must find it with your heart,
Never Never Land.

It might be miles beyond the moon,
Or right there where you stand.
Just keep an open mind,
And then suddenly, you'll find:
Never Never Land.

Refrain:
You'll have a treasure if you stay there,
More precious far than gold.
For once you have found your way there,
You can never, never grow old.

And that's my home where dreams are born
And time is never planned.
Just think of lovely things,
And your heart will fly on wings,
Forever in Never Never Land.

Refrain

So come with me where dreams are born,
And time is never planned.
Just think of lovely things,
And your heart will fly on wings,
Forever in Never Never Land.

Never Will I Marry

By Frank Loesser

from *Greenwillow*

Any flimsy dimsy looking for true love
Better smile me no good, dearie, good day.
Any flimsy dimsy looking for true love
Better look her looking some other way,
For my kiss can be no evermore promise,
But a fancy dancy fiddle and free.
Any flimsy dimsy looking for true love
Better waste no time, no time on me.

Never, never will I marry,
Never, never will I wed.
Born to wander solitary,
Wide my world, narrow my bed.
Never, never, never will I marry,
Born to wander 'til I'm dead.

No burdens to bear,
No conscience nor care,
No mem'ries to mourn,
No turning, for I was:

Born to wander solitary,
Wide my world, narrow my bed.
Never, never, never will I marry,
Born to wander 'til I'm dead.

Nobody Makes a Pass at Me

Words and Music by Harold Rome

from *Pins and Needles*

I want men that I can squeeze,
That I can please, that I can tease.
Two or three or four or more!
What are those fools waiting for?

I want love and I want kissing,
I want more of what I'm missing.
Nobody comes knocking at my front door.
What do they think my knocker's for?
If they don't come soon,
   there won't be any more!
What can the matter be?

I wash my clothes with Lux,
My etiquette's the best,
I spend my hard-earned bucks
On just what the ads suggest.

Refrain:
Oh dear, what can the matter be?
Nobody makes a pass at me!

I'm full of Kellogg's bran,
Eat grapenuts on the sly,
A date is on the can
Of the coffee that I buy.

Refrain

Oh, Beatrice Fairfax,
Give me the bare facts,
How do you make them fall?
If you don't save me,
The things the Lord gave me,
Never will be any use to me at all.

I sprinkle on a dash
Of "Fragrance de Amour,"
The ads say, "Makes Men Rash,"
But I guess their smell is poor.

Refrain

I use Ovaltine and Listerine,
Barbasol and Musterole,
Life Buoy soap and Flit,
So why ain't I got it?

I use Coca Cola and Marmola,
Crisco, Lesco and Mazola,
Exlax and Vapex,
So why ain't I got sex?

I use Albolene and Maybellene,
Alka Seltzer, Bromo Seltzer,
Odorono and Sensation,
So why ain't I got fascination?

My girdles come from Best,
The Times ads say they're chic,
And up above I'm dressed
In the brassiere of the week.

Refrain

I use Pond's on my skin,
With rye-crisp I have thinned,
I get my culture in,
I began "Gone with the Wind."

Refrain

Oh Dor'thy Dix, please,
Show me some tricks, please,
I want some men to hold.
I want attention
And things I won't mention,
And I want them all before I get too old.

I use Mum ev'ry day
And Angelus Liplure,
But still men stay away,
Just like Iv'ry soap, I'm pure.

Refrain

Nothing

Words by Edward Kleban
Music by Marvin Hamlisch

from *A Chorus Line*

Spoken:
I mean, I was dying to be a serious actress.
Anyway, it's the first day of acting class,
And we're in the auditorium
And the teacher, Mister Karp,
Puts us up on the stage
With our legs around everybody,
One in back of the other,
And he says: O.K., we're gonna do
    improvisations.
Now, you're on a bobsled and it's
    snowing out.
And it's cold. O.K., go!

Sung:
Ev'ry day for a week
We would try to feel the motion,
Feel the motion,
Down the hill.
Ev'ry day for a week
We would try to hear the wind rush,
Hear the wind rush,
Feel the chill.

And I dug right down to the bottom
    of my soul,
To see what I had inside.
Yes, I dug right down to the bottom
    of my soul,
And I tried; I tried.

Spoken:
Everyone is going:
Whoosh! I feel the snow,
I feel the cold—the air.
And Mr. Karp turns to me and says:
O.K., Morales, what did you feel?

Sung:
And I said, "Nothing,
I'm feeling nothing,"
And he says, "Nothing
Could get a girl transferred!"
They all felt something,
But I felt nothing,
Except the feeling
That this bullshit was absurd!

Spoken:
But I said to myself:
"Hey, it's only the first week.
Maybe it's genetic.
They don't have bobsleds in San Juan."

Sung:
Second week, more advanced,
And we had to be a table,
Be a sports car,
Ice cream cone.
Mister Karp, he would say,
"Very good, except Morales.
Try, Morales.
All alone."

So I dug right down to the bottom
    of my soul,
To see how an ice cream felt.
Yes, I dug right down to the bottom
    of my soul,
And I tried to melt.

The kids yelled, "Nothing!"
They called me "Nothing!"
And Karp allowed it,
Which really makes me burn.
They were so helpful,
They called me hopeless,
Until I really didn't know
Where else to turn!

Spoken:
And Karp kept saying,
"Morales, I think you should
Transfer to girls' high.
You'll never be an actress. Never!"
Jesus Christ!

Sung:
Went to church praying,
"Santa Maria, send me guidance,
Send me guidance."
On my knees.
Went to church praying,
"Santa Maria, help me feel it,
Help me feel it.
Pretty please!"

And a voice from down at the bottom
    of my soul,
Came up to the top of my head.
And the voice from down at the bottom
    of my soul,
Here is what it said:

"This man is nothing!
This course is nothing!
If you want something,
Go find a better class.
And when you find one,
You'll be an actress."
And I assure you that's what
Fin'lly came to pass.

Six months later I heard that Karp had died.
And I dug right down to the bottom
    of my soul,
And cried,
'Cause I felt—nothing.

On a Clear Day (You Can See Forever)

Words by Alan Jay Lerner
Music by Burton Lane

from *On a Clear Day You Can See Forever*

On a clear day,
Rise and look around you,
And you'll see who you are.
On a clear day,
How it will astound you,
That the glow of your being
Outshines every star.

You feel part of
Every mountain, sea and shore.
You can hear,
From far and near,
A world you've never heard before.
And on a clear day,
On that clear day,
You can see forever
And ever and ever and evermore!

On My Own

Music by Claude-Michel Schönberg
Lyrics by Alain Boublil, Herbert Kretzmer, John Caird, Trevor Nunn and Jean-Marc Natel

from *Les Misérables*

On my own, pretending he's beside me.
All alone, I walk with him 'til morning.
Without him, I feel his arms around me.
And when I lose my way,
I close my eyes and he has found me.

In the rain, the pavement shines like silver.
All the lights are misty in the river.
In the darkness the trees are full of starlight.
And all I see is him and me forever and forever.

And I know it's only in my mind
That I'm talking to myself and not to him.
And although I know that he is blind,
Still I say there's a way for us.

I love him, but when the night is over,
He is gone, the river's just a river.
Without him the world around me changes.
The trees are bare
And everywhere the streets are full of strangers.

I love him but every day I'm learning,
All my life I've only been pretending.
Without me his world will go on turning.
The world is full of happiness that I have never known.

I love him,
I love him,
I love him,
But only on my own.

On the Street Where You Live

Words by Alan Jay Lerner
Music by Frederick Loewe

from *My Fair Lady*

I have often walked
Down this street before
But the pavement always stayed beneath my feet before.
All at once am I,
Several stories high,
Knowing I'm on the street where you live.

Are there lilac trees
In the heart of town?
Can you hear a lark in any other part of town?
Does enchantment pour
Out of every door?
No, it's just on the street where you live.

And oh, the towering feeling,
Just to know somehow you are near!
The overpowering feeling
That any second you may suddenly appear!

People stop and stare,
They don't bother me;
For there's nowhere else on earth that I would rather be.

Let the time go by,
I won't care if I
Can be here on the street where you live.

On the Willows

Words and Music by Stephen Schwartz

from the Musical *Godspell*

Refrain:
On the willows there,
We hung up our lyres.
For our captors there
Required of us songs,
And our tormentors, mirth.

Refrain

Saying,
"Sing us one of the songs of Zion,
Sing us one of the songs of Zion,
Sing us one of the songs of Zion,"
But how can we sing,
Sing the Lord's song,
In a foreign land?

On the willows there,
We hung up our lyres.

Once in a Lifetime

Words and Music by Leslie Bricusse and Anthony Newley

from the musical production *Stop the World—I Want to Get Off*

Just once in a lifetime.
A man knows a moment
One wonderful moment
When fate takes his hand.
And this is my moment
My once in a lifetime
When I can explore
A new and exciting land.

For once in a lifetime
I feel like a giant.
I soar like an eagle
As tho' I had wings;
For this is my moment,
My destiny calls me,
And tho' it may be just once in a lifetime
I'm going to do great things.

Out of My Dreams

Lyrics by Oscar Hammerstein II
Music by Richard Rodgers

from *Oklahoma!*

Refrain:
Out of my dreams and into your arms I long to fly.
I will come as evening comes to woo a waiting sky.
Out of my dreams and into the hush of falling shadows,
When the mist is low and stars are breaking through,
Then out of my dreams I'll go
Into a dream with you.

Won't have to make up any more stories, you'll be there!
Think of the bright midsummer night glories we can share.
Won't have to go on kissing a daydream, I'll have you.
You'll be real, real as the white moon lighting the blue.

Refrain

People

Words by Bob Merrill
Music by Jule Styne

from *Funny Girl*

We travel single, O,
Maybe we're lucky,
But I don't know.
With them, just let one kid fall down
And seven mothers faint.
I guess we're both happy,
But maybe we ain't.

People, people who need people
Are the luckiest people in the world.
We're children, needing other children,
And yet letting our grown-up pride
Hide all the need inside,
Acting more like children, than children.
Lovers are very special people,
They're the luckiest people in the world.
With one person, one very special person,
A feeling deep in your soul says:
You were half now you're whole.
No more hunger and thirst, but first,
Be a person who needs people.
People who need people
Are the luckiest people in the world.

People Will Say We're in Love

Lyrics by Oscar Hammerstein II
Music by Richard Rodgers

from *Oklahoma!*

Verse (Girl):
Why do they think up stories that link my
   name with yours?
Why do the neighbors chatter all day,
   behind their doors?
I know a way to prove what they say is
   quite untrue.
Here is the gist, a practical list of "don'ts"
   for you.

Refrain:
Don't throw bouquets at me,
Don't please my folks too much,
Don't laugh at my jokes too much—
People will say we're in love!

Don't sigh and gaze at me,
Your sighs are so like mine,
You eyes mustn't glow like mine—
People will say we're in love!

Don't start collecting things
Give me my rose and glove;
Sweetheart, they're suspecting things—
People will say we're in love!

Verse 2 (Boy):
Some people claim that you are to blame
   as much as I.
Why do you take the trouble to bake
   my fav'rite pie?
Grantin' your wish, I carved our initials
   on the tree!
Jist keep a slice of all the advice you give
   so free.

Refrain 2:
Don't praise my charm too much,
Don't look so vain with me,
Don't stand in the rain with me—
People will say we're in love!

Don't take my arm too much,
Don't keep your hand in mine.
You hand looks so grand in mine,
People will say we're in love!

Don't dance all night with me,
Till the stars fade from above.
They'll see it's all right with me,
People will say we're in love!

Promises, Promises

Lyric by Hal David
Music by Burt Bacharach

from *Promises, Promises*

Promises, promises,
I'm all through with
Promises, promises now.
I don't know how
I got the nerve
To walk out.
If I shout,
Remember,
I feel free.
Now I can look at myself,
And be proud.
I'm laughing out loud,

Oh, promises, promises,
This is where those
Promises, promises end.
I won't pretend
That what was wrong
Can be right,
Ev'ry night
I'll sleep now.
No more lies.
Things that I promised myself
Fell apart,
But I found my heart.

Promises,
Their kind of promises
Can just destroy your life.
Oh, promises,
Those kind of promises
Take all the joy from life.
Oh, promises, promises,
My kind of promises
Can lead to joy,
And hope,
And love,
Yes, love!

Satin Doll

Words by Johnny Mercer and Billy Strayhorn
Music by Duke Ellington

from *Sophisticated Ladies*

Cigarette holder
Which wigs me
Over her shoulder,
She digs me
Out cattin' that satin doll.

Baby shall we go
Out skippin'
Careful amigo,
You're flippin'
Speaks Latin that satin doll.

She's nobody's fool,
So I'm playing it cool as can be,
I'll give it a whirl,
But I ain't for no girl catching me.

Spoken:
Switch-E-Rooney

Sung:
Telephone numbers well you know,
Doing my rhumbas with uno,
And that 'n' my satin doll.

Push de Button

Lyric by E.Y. Harburg
Music by Harold Arlen

from *Jamaica*

There's a little island on the Hudson,
Mythical, magic and fair,
Shining like a diamon' on de Hudson,
Far away from worriment and care.
What an isle, what an isle,
All the natives relax there in style.
What a life, what a life,
All de money controlled by de wife.

On this little island on de Hudson,
Ev'ryone big millionaire.
With his own cooporative castle,
Rising in de air conditioned air.
Life is easy,
Livin's lazy,
On this isle where crazy dreams come true.
All you do is:

Push de button,
Up de elevator,
Push de button,
Out de orange juice,
Push de button,
From refrigerator
Come banana short cake
And frozen goose.

Push de button,
Wipe de window wiper,
Push de button,
Rinse de baby diaper.
Push de button,
Wanna fry de fish,
Push de button,
Wash de dish,
Push de button,
Pooosh—
De button.

What an isle,
What an isle.
Where de automat feed ev'ry chile.
Where de brave
And de free
Live and love electronically.

Push de button,
Don't be small potatah.
Be a tycoon,
Big manipulatah.

Refrain:
Pooosh,
Apply de little finger and
Pooosh—
De button.

Push de button,
Up de helicopter,
Push de button,
Click de telephone.
Push de button,
From de television
Come de Pepto Bismo
With baritone.

Push de button,
Out come Pagliacci,
Push de button,
Also Liberace.
Push de button,
Wan to rock 'n' roll,
Push de button,
Cococol',
Push de button,
Pooosh—
De button.

What an isle,
What an isle.
Squeeze de tube and get Pepsodent smile.
Crack de bank,
Rob de mail.
Turn de knob and get Muzak in jail.

Push de button,
Don't be antiquated.
Get de baby
All prefabricated.

Refrain

Reviewing the Situation

Words and Music by Lionel Bart

from the Broadway Musical *Oliver!*

A man's got a heart, hasn't he?
Joking apart—hasn't he?
And tho' I'd be the first one to say
That I wasn't a saint—
I'm finding it hard to be really
As black as they paint.

I'm reviewing the situation.
Can a fellow be a villain all his life?
All the trials and tribulation,
Better settle down and get myself a wife.

And a wife could cook and sew for me,
And come for me and go for me,
(And go for me,)
And nag at me,
The fingers she will wag at me,
The money she will take from me,
A misery, she'll make from me—
I think I'd better think it out again.

A wife you can keep, anyway.
I'd rather sleep, anyway,
Left without anyone in the world
And I'm starting from now—
So how to win friends
And to influence people, so how?

I'm reviewing the situation.
I must quickly look up ev'ryone I know,
Titled people with a station,
Who can help me make a real
    impressive show.

I will own a suite at Claridges,
And run a fleet of carriages,
And wave at all the Duchesses
With friendliness,
As much as is befitting of my new estate.
"Good morrow to you, Magistrate!"
I think I'd better think it out again.

So, where shall I go?
Somebody?
Who do I know?
Nobody?
All my dearest companions have
Always been villains and thieves—
So at my time of life I should
Start turning over new leaves.

I'm reviewing the situation.
If you want to eat you've got to earn a bob!
Is it such a humiliation
For a robber to perform an honest job?

So a job I'm getting possibly,
I wonder how the boss'll be?
I wonder if he'll take to me?
What bonuses he'll make to me?
I'll start at eight, and finish late,
At normal rate and all, but wait!
I think I'd better think it out again.

What happens if I'm seventy?
Must come a time—seventy,
When you're old and it's cold
And who cares if you live or you die.
Your one consolation's
The money you may have put by.

I'm reviewing the situation,
I'm a bad 'un and a bad 'un I shall stay!
You'll be seeing no transformation,
But it's wrong to be a rogue in ev'ry way.

I don't want nobody hurt for me,
Or made to do the dirt for me.
This rotten life is not for me.
It's getting far too hot for me.
Don't want no one to rob for me,
But who will find a job for me?
I don't care what they've got for me.
But who will change the plot for me?
I think I'll have to think it out again.
Hey!

The Saga of Jenny

Words by Ira Gershwin
Music by Kurt Weill

from the Musical Production *Lady in the Dark*

There once was a girl named Jenny,
Whose virtues were varied and many,
Excepting that she was inclined
Always to make up her mind,
And Jenny points a moral
With which you cannot quarrel,
As you will find.

Jenny made her mind up when she
    was three,
She, herself, was going to trim the
    Christmas tree;
Christmas Eve she lit the candles,
    tossed the tapers away.
Little Jenny was an orphan on Christmas Day.

Poor Jenny! Bright as a penny!
Her equal would be hard to find.
She lost one dad and mother,
A sister and a brother,
But she would make up her mind.

Jenny made her mind up when she
    was twelve,
That into foreign languages she would delve,
But at seventeen to Vassar it was quite a blow
That in twenty-seven languages she couldn't
    say no.

Poor Jenny! Bright as a penny!
Her equal would be hard to find.
To Jenny I'm beholden,
Her heart was big and golden,
But she would make up her mind.

Jenny made her mind up at twenty-two,
To get herself a husband was the thing to do,
She got herself all dolled up in
    her satins and furs,
And she got herself a husband,
    but he wasn't hers.

Poor Jenny! Bright as a penny!
Her equal would be hard to find.
Deserved a bed of roses,
But history discloses,
That she would make up her mind.

Jenny made her mind up at thirty-nine,
She would take a trip to the Argentine.
She was only on vacation,
    but the Latins agree,
Jenny was the one who started the
    Good Neighbor Policy.

Poor Jenny! Bright as a penny!
Her equal would be hard to find.
Oh, passion doesn't vanish,
In Portugese or Spanish,
But she would make up her mind.

Jenny made her mind up at fifty-one,
She would write her memoirs before
    she was done,
The very day her book was published
    history relates
There were wives who shot their husbands
In some thirty-three states.

Poor Jenny! Bright as a penny!
Her equal would be hard to find.
She could give cards and spadies,
To many other ladies,
But she would make up her mind.

Jenny made her mind up at seventy-five,
She would live to be the oldest
    woman alive,
But gin and rum and destiny play
    funny tricks
And poor Jenny kicked the bucket
    at seventy-six.

Jenny points a moral,
With which you cannot quarrel,
Makes a lot of common sense.
Jenny and her saga,
Prove that you are gaga,
If you don't keep sitting on the fence.

Jenny and her story point the way to glory,
To all men and woman kind.
Anyone with a vision, comes to this decision,
Don't make up, you shouldn't make up,
You mustn't make up, oh never make up
Anyone with a vision, comes to this decision,
Don't make up your mind!

Sentimental Me

Words by Lorenz Hart
Music by Richard Rodgers

from the Broadway Musical *The Garrick Gaieties*

Look at me again, dear,
Let's hold hands and then, dear,
Sigh in chorus,
It won't bore us, to be sure.
There's no meaning to it,
Yet we overdo it,
With a relish
That is hellish to endure.
I am not the kind that merely flirts,
I just love and love until it hurts.

Oh, sentimental me and poor romantic you,
Dreaming dreams is all that we can do.
We hang around all day and ponder,
While both of us grow fonder,
The Lord knows where we're wandering to!

I sit and sigh, you sigh and sit upon my knee,
We laugh and cry, and never disagree.
A million kisses we'll make theft of,
Until there's nothing left of
Poor romantic you and sentimental me.

Shadowland

Music by Lebo M and Hans Zimmer
Lyrics by Mark Mancina and Lebo M

from Disney Presents *The Lion King: The Broadway Musical*

Chorus:
Refrain:
Fatshe leso lea halalela.
Fatshe leso lea halalela.

Nala:
Shadowland,
The leaves have fallen.
This shadowed land,
This was our home.

The river's dry,
The ground has broken.
So I must go,
Now I must go.

And where the journey may lead me,
Let your prayers be my guide.
I cannot stay here, my family,
But I'll remember my pride.

Chorus:
Prideland,
My land,
Tearstained
Dry land.
Take this with you,
Fatshe leso.

Nala:
I have no choice.
I will find my way.
Lea halalela.
Take this prayer,
What lies out there.
Lea halalela.

Chorus:
And where the journey may lead you,
Let this prayer be your guide.
Though it may take you so far away,
Always remember your pride.

Refrain

Nala:
Mm. Gigiza buyabo.
Besibo, my people, Besibo.

She (He) Touched Me

Lyric by Ira Levin
Music by Milton Schafer

from *Drat! The Cat!*

*Note: Though the original lyric was "She Touched Me," the song has become best
known as "He Touched Me" due to Barbra Streisand's recording.*

She (He) touched me,
She (He) put her hand near mine and then
She (He) touched me.
I felt a sudden tingle when she (he) touched me,
A sparkle, a glow!

She (He) knew it,
It wasn't accidental,
No, she (he) knew it.
She (He) smiled and seemed to tell me so all through it,
She (He) knew it, I know.

She's (He's) real and the world is alive and shining.
I feel such a wonderful drive toward valentining.
She (He) touched me, I simply have to face the fact,
She (He) touched me.
Control myself and try to act as if I remember my name.
But she (he) touched me,
She (He) touched me,
And suddenly nothing is the same.

Show Me

Words by Alan Jay Lerner
Music by Frederick Loewe

from *My Fair Lady*

Words! Words! Words!
I'm so sick of words!
I get words all day through,
First from him, now from you!
Is that all you blighters can do?

Don't talk of stars burning above,
If you're in love, show me!
Tell me no dreams filled with desire,
If you're on fire, show me!

Here we are together in the middle
    of the night!
Don't talk of spring! Just hold me tight!
Anyone who's ever been in love'll
    tell you that
This is no time for a chat!

Haven't your lips longed for my touch?
Don't say how much, show me!
Show me!
Don't talk of love lasting through time.
Make me no undying vow.
Show me now.

Sing me no song! Read me no rhyme!
Don't waste my time; show me!
Don't talk of June! Don't talk of fall!
Don't talk at all; show me!

Never do I ever want to hear another word.
There isn't one I haven't heard.
Here we are together in what ought
    to be a dream,
Say one more word and I'll scream!

Haven't your arms hungered for mine?
Please don't expl'in, show me!
Show me!
Don't wait until wrinkles and lines
Pop out all over my brow.
Show me now.

Siberia

Words and Music by Cole Porter

from *Silk Stockings*

When we're sent to dear Siberia,
To Si-ber-i-eer-i-a,
When it's cocktail time, 'twill be so nice,
Just to know you'll not have to phone for ice.

When we meet in sweet Siberia,
Far from communist hysteria,
We'll go on a tear,
For our buddies all are there,
In cheery Siberia.

When we're sent to dear Siberia,
To Si-ber-i-eer-i-a,
Where they say all day the sun shines bright,
And they also say that it shines all night.

The aurora borealis is
Not as heated as a palace is,
If on heat you dote,
You can shoot a sable coat,
In cheery Siberia.

When we're sent to dear Siberia,
To Si-ber-i-eer-i-a,
Where the labor laws are all so fair
That you never have unemployment there.

When we meet in sweet Siberia,
To protect us from diphtheria,
We can toast our toes
On the lady Eskimos,
In cheery Siberia.

When we're sent to dear Siberia,
To Si-ber-i-eer-i-a,
Since the big salt mines will be so near,
We can all have salt to put in our beer.

When we meet in sweet Siberia,
Where the snow is so superia,
You can bet, all right,
That your Christmas will be white,
In cheery Siberia.

Small World

Words by Stephen Sondheim
Music by Jule Styne

from *Gypsy*

Funny, you're a stranger who's come here,
Come from another town.
Funny, I'm a stranger myself here.
Small world, isn't it?

Funny, you're a girl who goes traveling,
Rather than settling down.
Funny, 'cause I'd love to go traveling.
Small world, isn't it?

We have so much in common,
It's a phenomenon.
We could pool our resources
By joining forces from now on.

Lucky, you're a girl who likes children,
That's an important sign.
Lucky, 'cause I'd love to have children.
Small world, isn't it? Funny, isn't it?
Small and funny and fine.

So in Love

Words and Music by Cole Porter

from *Kiss Me, Kate*

Strange, dear, but true, dear,
When I'm close to you, dear,
The stars fill the sky,
So in love with you am I.

Even without you,
My arms fold about you.
You know, darling, why.
So in love with you am I.

In love with the night mysterious,
The night when you first were there.
In love with my joy delirious,
When I knew that you could care.

So taunt me, and hurt me,
Deceive me, desert me.
I'm yours 'til I die.
So in love,
So in love,
So in love with you, my love, am I.

Solitude

Words and Music by Duke Ellington, Eddie De Lange and Irving Mills

from *Sophisticated Ladies*

In my solitude you haunt me
With reveries of days gone by.
In my solitude you taunt me
With memories that never die.
I sit in my chair,
Filled with despair,
Nobody could be so sad.
With gloom everywhere
I sit and stare,
I know that I'll soon go mad.
In my solitude,
I'm praying
Dear Lord above,
Send back my love.

Some Enchanted Evening

Lyrics by Oscar Hammerstein II
Music by Richard Rodgers

from *South Pacific*

Some enchanted evening
You may see a stranger,
You may see a stranger
Across a crowded room.
And somehow you know,
You know even then,
That somewhere you'll see her again
    and again.

Some enchanted evening
Someone may be laughing,
You may hear her laughing
Across a crowded room—
And night after night,
As strange as it seems,
The sound of her laughter will sing in
    your dreams.

Who can explain it?
Who can tell you why?
Fools give you reasons—
Wise men never try.

Some enchanted evening
When you find your true love,
When you hear her call you
Across a crowded room,
Then fly to her side
And make her your own,
Or all through your life
You may dream all alone.
Once you have found her,
Never let her go.
Once you have found her,
Never let her go.

Somebody Loves Me

Words by B.G. DeSylva and Ballard MacDonald
Music by George Gershwin
French Version by Emelia Renaud

from *George White's Scandals of 1924*

When this old world began
It was heaven's plan.
There should be a girl for every single man.
To my great regret
Someone has upset,
Heaven's pretty program for we've never met.
I'm clutching at straws,
Just because
I may meet her yet.

Refrain:
Somebody loves me
I wonder who,
I wonder who she can be.
Somebody loves me
I wish I knew,
Who can she be worries me.
For every girl who passes me I shout, Hey! maybe
You were meant to be my loving baby.
Somebody loves me
I wonder who,
Maybe it's you.

Repeat Refrain

Somebody, Somewhere

By Frank Loesser

from *The Most Happy Fella*

Wanting to be wanted,
Needing to be needed,
That's what it is.
That's what it is.
Now I'm lucky that:

Somebody, somewhere
Wants me and needs me,
That's very wonderful
To know.

Somebody lonely
Wants me to care,
Wants me of all people
To notice him there.

Well, I want to be wanted,
Need to be needed,
And I'll admit I'm all
Aglow.

'Cause somebody, somewhere
Wants me and needs me,
Wants lonely me to smile
And say, "Hello."

Somebody, somewhere
Wants me and needs me,
And that's very wonderful
To know.

Sorry-Grateful

Music and Lyrics by Stephen Sondheim

from *Company*

You're always sorry,
You're always grateful,
You're always wond'ring
What might have been.
Then she walks in.

And still you're sorry,
And still you're grateful,
And still you wonder,
And still you doubt,
And she goes out.

Ev'rything's diff'rent,
Nothing's changed,
Only maybe slightly
Rearranged.

Refrain:
You're sorry-grateful,
Regretful-happy.
Why look for answers
Where none occur?

You always are
What you always were,
Which has nothing to do with,
All to do with her.

You're always sorry,
You're always grateful,
You hold her, thinking,
"I'm not alone."
You're still alone.

You don't live for her,
You do live with her.
You're scared she's starting
To drift away,
And scared she'll stay.

Good things get better,
Bad get worse.
Wait, I think I meant that
In reverse.

Refrain

You'll always be
What you always were,
Which has nothing to do with,
All to do with her.

Soon It's Gonna Rain

Words by Tom Jones
Music by Harvey Schmidt

from *The Fantasticks*

She:
Hear how the wind begins to whisper.
See how the leaves go streaming by.
Smell how the velvet rain is falling,
Out where the fields are warm and dry.
Now is the time to run inside and stay.
Now is the time to find a hideaway,
Where we can stay.

He:
Soon it's gonna rain;
I can see it.
Soon it's gonna rain;
I can tell.
Soon it's gonna rain.
What are we gonna do?

Soon it's gonna rain;
I can feel it.
Soon it's gonna rain;
I can tell.
Soon it's gonna rain.
What'll we do with you?

We'll find four limbs of a tree.
We'll bind four walls and a floor.
We'll bind it over with leaves,
And duck inside to stay.

Both:
Then we'll let it rain.
We'll not feel it.
Then we'll let it rain.
Rain pell-mell.
And we'll not complain
If it never stops at all.
We'll live and love,
Within our own four walls.

He:
We'll find four limbs of a tree.
We'll bind four walls and a floor.
We'll bind it over with leaves,
And run inside to stay.
(Soon it's gonna rain.)
Come run inside to stay.
(Soon it's gonna rain.)

Soon it's gonna rain;
I can see it.
I can feel it.
Run inside. And—

He:
Then we'll let it rain.
We'll not feel it.
And we'll not complain
If it never stops at all.

She:
Then we'll let it rain.
Then we'll let it rain.
Happy ending,
Then we'll let it rain.

She:
Why complain?
We'll live and love within our wall.
He:
Happily we'll live and love,
No cares at all.

Both:
Happily we'll live and love,
Within our castle wall.

The Sound of Music

Lyrics by Oscar Hammerstein II
Music by Richard Rodgers

from *The Sound of Music*

My day in the hills has come to an end, I know.
A star has come out to tell me it's time to go,
But deep in the dark-green shadows
Are voices that urge me to stay.
So I pause and I wait and I listen
For one more sound,
For one more lovely thing
That the hills might say…

The hills are alive
With the sound of music,
With songs they have sung
For a thousand years.
The hills fill my heart
With the sound of music—
My heart wants to sing
Every song it hears.

My heart wants to beat
Like the wings of the birds that rise
From the lake to the trees.
My heart wants to sigh like a chime that flies
From a church on a breeze,
To laugh like a brook when it trips and falls
Over stones in its way,
To sing through the night
Like a lark that is learning to pray—

I go to the hills when my heart is lonely,
I know I will hear what I've heard before.
My heart will be blessed with the sound of music
And I'll sing once more.

Stars

Music by Claude-Michel Schönberg
Lyrics by Herbert Kretzmer and Alain Boublil

from *Les Misérables*

There, out in the darkness,
A fugitive running,
Fallen from grace,
Fallen from grace.
God be my witness,
I never shall yield,
Till we come face to face,
Till we come face to face.

He knows his way in the dark,
But mine is the way of the Lord.
And those who follow the path
Of the righteous shall have their reward.
And if they fall, as Lucifer fell,
The flame, the sword!

Stars, in your multitudes,
Scarce to be counted,
Filling the darkness,
With order and light.
You are the sentinels,
Silent and sure,
Keeping watch in the night,
Keeping watch in the night.

You know your place in the skies,
You hold your course and your aim.
And each in your season returns and returns,
And is always the same.
And if you fall, as Lucifer fell,
You fall in flame!

And so it has been,
And so it is written
On the doorways to paradise,
That those who falter
And those who fall
Must pay the price.

Lord, let me find him,
That I may see him,
Safe behind bars!
I will never rest 'til then.
This I swear!
This I swear by the stars.

Stranger in Paradise

Words and Music by Robert Wright and George Forrest
(Music Based on Themes of A. Borodin)

from *Kismet*

Marsinah:
Oh, why do the leaves of the mulberry tree
Whisper diff'rently now?
And why is the nightingale singing at noon
On the mulberry bough?
For some most mysterious reason,
This isn't the garden I know.
No, it's paradise now,
That was only a garden a moment ago.

Caliph:
Take my hand,
I'm a stranger in paradise.
All lost in a wonderland,
A stranger in paradise.

If I stand starry eyed,
That's a danger in paradise,
For mortals who stand beside
An angel like you.

Refrain:
I saw your face,
And I ascended,
Out of the commonplace,
Into the rare!
Somewhere in space,
I hang suspended,
Until I know
There's a chance that you care.

Won't you answer the fervent pray'r
Of a stranger in paradise?
Don't send me in dark despair
From all that I hunger for.

But open your angel's arms
To the stranger in paradise,
And tell him that he need be
A stranger no more.

Marsinah:
Refrain

Caliph:
Somewhere in space,
I hang suspended,
Till the moment I know
There's a chance that you care.

Marsinah:
Won't you answer the fervent pray'r
Of a stranger in paradise?
Caliph:
Don't send me in dark despair
From all that I hunger for.

Both:
But open your angel's arms
To the stranger in paradise,
And tell me that I need be
A stranger no more.

Sun and Moon

Music by Claude-Michel Schönberg
Lyrics by Richard Maltby Jr. and Alain Boublil
Adapted from original French Lyrics by Alain Boublil

from *Miss Saigon*

You are sunlight and I moon,
Joined by the gods of fortune,
Midnight and high noon,
Sharing the sky.
We have been blessed, you and I.

You are here like a myst'ry.
I'm from a world that's so diff'rent
From all that you are.
How in the light of one night
Did we come so far?

Outside, day starts to dawn.
Your moon still floats on high.
The birds awake.
The stars shine, too.
My hands still shake,
I reach for you,
And we meet in the sky.

You are sunlight and I moon,
Joined here bright'ning the sky
With the flame of love.
Made of sunlight, moonlight.

Supper Time

Words and Music by Irving Berlin

from the Stage Production *As Thousands Cheer*

Supper time,
I should set the table 'cause it's supper time.
Somehow I'm not able 'cause that man o'mine
Ain't comin' home no more.

Supper time,
Kids will soon be yellin' for their supper time.
How'll I keep from tellin' that that man o'mine
Ain't comin' home no more.

How'll I keep explainin'
When they ask me where he's gone?
How'll I keep from cryin' when I bring their supper on?
How can I remind them to pray at their humble board?
How can I be thankful when they start to thank the Lord, Lord.

Supper time,
I should set the table 'cause it's supper time.
Somehow I'm not able 'cause that man o'mine
Ain't comin' home no more.
Ain't comin' home no more.

That'll Show Him

Words and Music by Stephen Sondheim

from *A Funny Thing Happened on the Way to the Forum*

Let the captain wed me and woo me,
I shall play my part!
Let him make his mad passion to me,
You will have my heart.
He can have the body he paid for,
Nothing but the body he paid for.
When he has the body he paid for,
Our revenge will start!

When I kiss him,
I'll be kissing you.
So I'll kiss him morning and night—
That'll show him!

When I hold him,
I'll be holding you,
So I'll hold him ten times as tight—
That'll show him too!

I shall coo and tenderly stroke his hair,
Wish that you were there,
You'd enjoy it!

When it's evening
And we're in our tent for two,
I'll sit on his knee,
Get to know him intimately,
That'll show him
How much I really love you!

The Surrey with the Fringe on Top

Lyrics by Oscar Hammerstein II
Music by Richard Rodgers

from *Oklahoma!*

When I take you out tonight with me,
Honey, here's the way it's goin' to be:
You will set behind a team of snow-white horses
In the slickest gig you ever see!

Chicks and ducks and geese better scurry
When I take you out in the surrey,
When I take you out in the surrey with the fringe on top.
Watch that fringe and see how it flutters
When I drive them high-steppin' strutters
Nosey-pokes'll peek through their shutters
And their eyes will pop!
The wheels are yeller, the upholstery's brown,
The dashboard's genuine leather,
With isinglass curtains you can roll right down
In case there's a change in the weather;
Two bright side lights winkin' and blinkin',
Aint no finer rig, I'm a-thinkin';
You c'n keep yer rig if you're thinkin' 'at I'd keer to swap
Fer that shiny little surrey with the fringe on the top.

Would y' say the fringe was made of silk?
Wouldn't have no other kind but silk.
Has it really got a team of snow-white horses?
One's like snow—the other's more like milk.

All the world'll fly in a flurry
When I take you out in the surrey,
When I take you out in the surrey with the fringe on top.
When we hit the road, hell for leather,
Cats and dogs'll dance in the heather,
Birds and frogs'll sing altogether,
And the toads will hop!
The wind'll whistle as we rattle along,
The cows'll moo in the clover,
The river will ripple out a whispered song,
And whisper it over and over:
Don't you wisht y'd go on ferever?
Don't you wisht y'd go on ferever?
Don't you wisht y'd go on ferever and ud never stop
In that shiny little surrey with the fringe on the top?

I can see the stars gittin' blurry
When we ride back home in the surrey,
Drivin' slowly home in the surrey with the fringe on top.
I can feel the day gittin' older,
Feel a sleepy head near my shoulder,
Noddin', droopin' close to my shoulder till it falls, kerplop!
The sun is swimmin' on the rim of a hill,
The moon is takin' a header,
And jist as I'm thinkin' all the earth is still,
A lark'll wake up in the medder...
Hush! You bird, my baby's a-sleepin'—
Maybe got a dream worth a-keepin'.
Whoa! You team, and jist keep a-creepin' at a slow clip-clop;
Don't you hurry with the surrey with the fringe on the top.

There's a Small Hotel

Words by Lorenz Hart
Music by Richard Rodgers

from *On Your Toes*

Frankie:
I'd like to get away, Junior,
Somewhere alone with you.
It could be oh, so gay, Junior!
You need a laugh or two.

Junior:
A certain place I know, Frankie,
Where funny people can have fun.
That's where we two will go, darling,
Before you can count up
One, two, three
For...

Refrain:
There's a small hotel
With a wishing well;
I wish that we were there
Together.
There's a bridal suite;
One room bright and neat,
Complete for us to share
Together.

Looking through the window
You can see a distant steeple;
Not a sign of people,
Who wants people?
When the steeple bell says,
"Goodnight, sleep well,"
We'll thank the small hotel
Together.

Refrain

Looking through the window
You can see a distant steeple;
Not a sign of people,
Who wants people?
When the steeple bell says,
"Goodnight, sleep well,"
We'll thank the small hotel.
We'll creep into our little shell
And we will thank the small hotel
Together.

They Didn't Believe Me

Words by Herbert Reynolds
Music by Jerome Kern

from *The Girl from Utah*

He:
Got the cutest little way,
Like to watch you all the day.
And it certainly seems fine
Just to think that you'll be mine.

When I see your pretty smile,
Makes the living worth the while.
So I've got to run around,
Telling people what I've found.

And when I told them
How beautiful you are,
They didn't believe me,
They didn't believe me!

Your lips, your eyes, your cheeks, your hair,
Are in a class beyond compare,
You're the loveliest girl
That one could see!

And when I tell them,
And I cert'nly am goin' to tell them,
That I'm the man whose wife one day
    you'll be,
They'll never believe me,
They'll never believe me,
That from this great big world you've
    chosen me!

She:
Don't know how it happened quite,
May have been the summer night,
May have been, well, who can say,
Things just happen any way,

All I know is I said, "Yes!"
Hesitating, more or less,
And you kissed me where I stood,
Just like any fellow would.

And when I told them
How wonderful you are,
They didn't believe me,
They didn't believe me!

Your lips, your eyes, your curly hair
Are in a class beyond compare,
You're the loveliest thing
That one could see!

And when I tell them,
And I cert'nly am goin' to tell them,
That I'm the girl whose boy one day
    you'll be,
They'll never believe me,
They'll never believe me,
That from this great big world you've
    chosen me!

There's No Business Like Show Business

Words and Music by Irving Berlin

from the Stage Production *Annie Get Your Gun*

The butcher, the baker, the grocer, the clerk
Are secretly unhappy men because
The butcher, the baker, the grocer, the clerk
Get paid for what they do but no applause.
They'd gladly bid their dreary jobs goodbye,
For anything theatrical and why.

There's no business like show business
Like no business I know.
Everything about it is appealing.
Everything the traffic will allow.
Nowhere could you get that happy feeling
When you are stealing
That extra bow.

There's no people like show people.
They smile when they are low.
Even with a turkey that you know will fold,
You may be stranded out in the cold.
Still you wouldn't change it for a sack of gold.
Let's go on with the show.

The costumes, the scenery, the make-up, the props,
The audience that lifts you up when you're down,
The headaches, the heartaches, the backaches, the flops
The sheriff who escorts you out of town.
The opening when your heart beats like a drum,
The closing when the customers won't come.

There's no business like show business
Like no business I know.
You get word before the show has started
That your favorite uncle died at dawn.
Top of that your Pa and Ma have parted,
You're broken-hearted but you go on.

There's no people like show people.
They don't run out of dough.
Angels come from everywhere with lots of jack.
And when you lose it, there's no attack.
Where could you get money that don't give back.
Let's go on with the show.

The cowboys, the tumblers, the wrestlers, the clowns,
The roustabouts who move the show at dawn,
The music, the spotlights, the people, the towns,
Your baggage with the labels pasted on.
The sawdust and the horses and the smell,
The towel you've taken from the last hotel.

There's no business like show business
Like no business I know.
Traveling through the country will be thrilling.
Standing out in front on opening nights.
Smiling as you watch the theatre filling,
And there's your billing out there in lights.

There's no people like show people.
They smile when they are low.
Yesterday they told you you would not go far.
That night you open and there you are.
Next day on your dressing room they've hung a star.
Let's go on with the show.

They Live in You

Music and Lyrics by Mark Mancina, Jay Rifkin and Lebo M

from Disney Presents *The Lion King: The Broadway Musical*

Ingonyama nengw' enamabala.
Ingonyama nengw' enamabala.

Night,
And the spirit of life,
Calling. Oh, oh, iyo.
Mamela. Oh, oh, iyo.

And a voice,
With the fear of a child,
Asking. Oh, oh, iyo.
Oh, mamela. Oh, oh, iyo.

Mamela, mamela iyo. Hela.
Wait,
There's no mountain too great.
Hear these words and have faith.
Oh, oh, oh iyo.
Have faith.
Hela hey mamela. Hela.

Refrain:
They live in you.
Hela hey mamela.
Hela. They live in me.
Hela hey mamela.
Hela. They're watching over.
Hela hey mamela.
Ev'rything we see.
Hela hey mamela.
In ev'ry creature.
Hela hey mamela.
In ev'ry star.
Hela hey mamela.
In your reflection,
They live in you.

Refrain

Ingonyama nengw' enamabala.

They Say It's Wonderful

Words and Music by Irving Berlin

from the Stage Production *Annie Get Your Gun*

Annie:
Rumors fly and you can't tell where
   they start,
'Specially when it concerns a person's heart.
I've heard tales that could set my
   heart a-glow.
Wish I knew if the things I hear are so.

They say that falling in love is wonderful,
It's wonderful so they say.
And with a moon up above,
It's wonderful,
It's wonderful so they tell me.

I can't recall who said it,
I know I never read it.
I only know they tell me that love is grand,
And the thing that's known as romance
   is wonderful,
Wonderful in every way,
So they say.

Frank:
Rumors fly and you often leave a doubt,
But you've come to the right place to
   find out.
Everything that you've heard is really so.
I've been there once or twice and
   I should know.

You'll find that falling in love is wonderful,
It's wonderful.

Annie:
So you say.

Frank:
And with a moon up above,
It's wonderful, it's wonderful.

Annie:
So you tell me.

Frank:
To leave your house some morning,
And without any warning,
You're stopping people
Shouting that love is grand.
And to hold a man in your arms is
   wonderful,
Wonderful in every way,

Annie:
So you say.

Thou Swell

Words by Lorenz Hart
Music by Richard Rodgers

from *A Connecticut Yankee*

Babe, we are well met,
As in a spell met;
I lift my helmet,
Sandy,
You're just dandy.
For just this here lad.
You're such a fistful,
My eyes are mistful;
Are you too wistful
To care?
Do say you care
To say, "Come near lad."
You are so graceful;
Have you wings?
You have a face full
Of nice things;
You have no speaking voice, dear,
With every word it sings.

Refrain:
Thou swell!
Thou witty!
Thou sweet!
Thou grand!
Wouldst kiss me pretty?
Wouldst hold my hand?
Both thine eyes are cute too;
What they do to me.
Hear me holler
I choose a
Sweet lollapalooza
In thee.

I'd feel so rich in
A hut for two
Two rooms and kitchen
I'm sure would do;
Give me just a plot of,
Not a lot of land
And,
Thou swell!
Thou witty!
Thou grand!

Thy words are queer, Sir,
Unto mine ear, Sir,
Yet thou'rt a dear, Sir,
To me.
Thou could'st woo me.
Now could'st thou try, knight.
I'd murmur "Swell" too,
And like it well too.
More thou wilt tell to
Sandy.
Thou art dandy;
Now art thou my knight.
Thine arms are martial,
Thou hast grace.
My cheek is partial
To they face.
And if thy lips grow weary,
Mine are their resting place.

Refrain

Till There Was You

By Meredith Willson

from Meredith Willson's *The Music Man*

There were bells
On the hill,
But I never heard them ringing.
No, I never heard them at all,
Till there was you.

There were birds
In the sky,
But I never saw them winging.
No, I never saw them at all,
Till there was you.

And there was music,
And there were wonderful roses,
They tell me,
In sweet fragrant meadows of dawn
And dew.

There was love
All around,
But I never heard it singing.
No, I never heard it at all,
Till there was you.

Together

Words and Music by B.G. DeSylva, Ray Henderson and Lew Brown

from *Good News!*

Refrain:
We strolled the lane,
Together,
Laughed at the rain,
Together,
Sang love's refrain,
Together.

And we'd both pretend
It would never end.

One day we cried,
Together,
Cast love aside,
Together.
You're gone from me,
But in my memory
We always will be
Together.

Refrain

We knew long ago
That our love would grow.

Through storm and sun,
Together.
Our hearts as one,
Together.
You're gone from me,
But in my memory
We always will be
Together.

Tschaikowsky (And Other Russians)

Words by Ira Gershwin
Music by Kurt Weill

from the Musical Production *Lady in the Dark*

There's Malichevsky, Rubenstein,
Arensky and Tschaikowsky,
Sapelnikoff, Dimitrieff,
Tscherepnin, Kryjanowsky,

Godowsky, Arteiboucheff,
Moniuszko, Akimenko,
Solovieff, Prokofieff,
Tiomkin, Korestchenko.

There's Glinka, Winkler, Bortniansky,
Rebikoff, Ilyinsky,
There's Medtner, Balakireff,
Zolotareff and Kvoschinsky.

And Sokoloff and Kopyloff,
Dukelsky and Klenofsky,
And Shostakovitsch, Borodine,
Gliere and Nowakofski.

There's Liadoff and Karganoff,
Markievitsch, Pantschenko,
And Dorgomyzski, Stcherbatcheff,
Scriabine, Vassilenko,

Stravinsky, Rimsky-Korsakoff,
Mussorgsky and Gretchaninoff
And Glazounoff and Caesar Cui,
Kalinikoff, Rachmaninoff,

Stravinsky and Gretchnaninoff,
Rumshinsky and Rachmaninoff,
I really have to stop,
The subject has been dwelt upon enough!

Stravinsky, Gretchnaninoff,
Kvoschinsky, Rachmaninoff!
I really have to stop,
Because you all have undergone enough!

Together Wherever We Go

Words by Stephen Sondheim
Music by Jule Styne

from *Gypsy*

Refrain
Rose:
Wherever we go,
Whatever we do,
We're gonna go through it
Together.

We may not go far,
But sure as a star,
Wherever we are,
It's together.

Wherever I go,
I know he goes.
Wherever I go,
I know she goes.
No fits, no fights,
No feuds and no egos,
Amigos,
Together!

Through thick and through thin,
All out or all in,
And whether it's win,
Place or show,
With you for me,
And me for you,
We'll muddle through
Whatever we do,
Together,
Wherever we go!

All:
Refrain

Rose:
Wherever we sleep,
Louise:
If prices are steep,
Herbie:
We'll always sleep cheaper
Together.

Rose:
Whatever the boat I row,
You row.
Herbie:
A duo!
Rose:
Whatever the row I hoe,
You hoe.
Louise:
A trio!
Rose:
And any I-O-U I owe,
You owe.
Herbie:
Who, me? Oh, no, you owe!
Louise:
No, we owe,
All:
Together!

All:
We all take the bow,
Rose:
Including the cow,

All:
Though bus'ness is lousy and slow.
Rose:
With Herbie's vim,
Louise's verve,
Herbie and Louise:
Now all we need
Is someone with nerve,
Rose:
Together,
Herbie and Louise:
Together,
Rose:
Wherever,
Herbie and Louise:
Wherever,
All:
Together,
Wherever we go!

Rose:
If I start to dance,
Herbie and Louise:
We both start to dance,
All:
And sometimes by chance,
We're together.

Rose:
If I sing B flat (Oh),
Louise:
We both hit B flat (Oh),
Herbie:
We all can be flat (Oh),
All:
Together!

Herbie:
Whatever the trick,
We can do it!
Louise:
With teamwork we're bound
To get through it.
Rose:
There really isn't anything to it.
You do it!
I knew it—
All:
We blew it,
Together!

All:
We go in a group,
We tour in a troupe,
We land in the soup,
But we know:
The things we do,
We do by threes,
A perfect team,
Rose:
No, this way, Louise!
Together,
Herbie and Louise:
Together,
Rose:
Wherever,
Herbie and Louise:
Wherever,
All:
Together,
Wherever we go!

Unusual Way (In a Very Unusual Way)

Words and Music by Maury Yeston

from *Nine*

In a very unusual way,
One time I needed you.
In a very unusual way,
You were my friend.
Maybe it lasted a day,
Maybe it lasted an hour,
But somehow it will never end.

In a very unusual way,
I think I'm in love with you.
In a very unusual way,
I want to cry.
Something inside me goes weak,
Something inside me surrenders,
And you're the reason why,
You're the reason why.

You don't know what you do to me,
You don't have a clue.
You can't tell what it's like to be me,
Looking at you.
It scares me so that I can hardly speak.

In a very unusual way,
I owe what I am to you.
Though at times it appears I won't stay,
I never go.
Special to me in my life,
Since the first day that I met you,
How could I ever forget you,
Once you had touched my soul?
In a very unusual way,
You've made me whole.

Wait Till You See Her

Words by Lorenz Hart
Music by Richard Rodgers

from *By Jupiter*

My friends who knew me
Never would know me,
They'd look right through me,
Above and below me
And ask, "Who's that man?
Who is that man?
That's not my lighthearted friend!"
Meeting one girl
Was the start of the end.
Love is a simple emotion
A friend should comprehend.

Wait till you see her,
See how she looks.
Wait till you hear her laugh.
Painters of paintings,
Writers of books,
Never could tell the half.
Wait till you feel
The warmth of her glance,
Pensive and sweet and wise.
All of it lovely,
All of it thrilling,
I'll never be willing to free her.
When you see her
You won't believe your eyes.

We Kiss in a Shadow

Lyrics by Oscar Hammerstein II
Music by Richard Rodgers

from *The King and I*

We kiss in a shadow,
We hide from the moon,
Our meetings are few
And over too soon.

We speak in a whisper,
Afraid to be heard,
When people are near,
We speak not a word.

Alone in our secret,
Together we sigh,
For one smiling day to be free,

To kiss in the sunlight,
And say to the sky:
Behold and believe what you see!
Behold how my lover loves me!

We Need a Little Christmas

Music and Lyric by Jerry Herman

from *Mame*

Haul out the holly,
Put up the tree before my—
Spirit falls again.
Fill up the stocking,
I may be rushing things, but—
Deck the halls again now.

For we need a little Christmas,
Right this very minute,
Candles in the window,
Carols at the spinet.
Yes, we need a little Christmas,
Right this very minute,
It hasn't snowed a single flurry,
But Santa, dear, we're in a hurry.

So climb down the chimney,
Turn on the brightest string of
Lights I've ever seen,
Slice up the fruitcake,
It's time we hung some tinsel
On that evergreen bough.

For I've grown a little leaner,
Grown a little colder,
Grown a little sadder,
Grown a little older.
And I need a little angel,
Sitting on my shoulder,
Need a little Christmas now!

For we need a little music,
Need a little laughter,
Need a little singing,
Ringing through the rafter.
And we need a little snappy
"Happy ever after,"
Need a little Christmas now!

Well, Did You Evah?

Words and Music by Cole Porter

from *DuBarry Was a Lady*

He:
When you're out in smart society,
And you suddenly get bad news,
You musn't show anxiety,
She:
And proceed to sing the blues.
He:
For example, tell me something bad,
Something awful, something grave,
And I'll show you how a Racquet Club lad
Would behave.

She:
Have you heard? The coast of Maine
Just got hit by a hurricane?
He:
Well, did you evah!
What a swell party this is!
She:
Have you heard that poor dear Blanche
Got run down by an avalanche?
He:
Well, did you evah!
What a swell party this is!
What daiquiris!
What sherry, please!
What Burgandy,
What great Pommery!
What brandy, wow!
What whiskey, here's how!
What gin and what beer!

She:
Will you sober up, my dear?
Have you heard Professor Munch
Ate his wife and divorced his lunch?
He:
Well, did you evah!
What a swell party this is!
She:
Missus Smith in her new Hup
Crossed the bridge when the bridge was up.
He:
Well, did you evah!
What a swell party this is!

ADDITIONAL LYRICS
Refrain 1
She:
Have you heard? The coast of Maine
Just got hit by a hurricane?
He:
Well, did you evah!
What a swell party this is!
She:
Have you heard that poor dear Blanche
Got run down by an avalanche?
He:
Well, did you evah!
What a swell party this is!
It's great, it's grand.
It's Wonderland!
It's tops, it's first.
It's DuPont, it's Hearst!

What soup, what fish.
That meat, what a dish!
What salad, what cheese!
She:
Pardon me one moment, please.
Have you heard that Uncle Newt
Forgot to open his parachute?
He:
Well, did you evah!
What a swell party this is!
She:
Old Aunt Susie just came back
With her child and the child is black.
He:
Well, did you evah!
What a swell party this is!

Refrain 2
He:
Have you heard it's in the stars
Next July we collide with Mars?
She:
Well, did you evah!
What a swell party this is!
He:
Have you heard that Grandma Doyle
Thought the Flit was her mineral oil?
She:
Well, did you evah!
What a swell party this is!
What daiquiris!
What sherry, please!
What Burgandy,
What great Pommery!

What brandy, wow!
What whiskey, here's how!
What gin and what beer!
He:
Will you sober up, my dear?
Have you heard Professor Munch
Ate his wife and divorced his lunch?
She:
Well, did you evah!
What a swell party this is!
He:
Have you heard that Mimmsie Starr
Just got pinched in the Astor Bar?
She:
Well, did you evah!
What a swell party this is!

Refrain 3
She:
Have you heard that poor old Ted
Just turned up in an oyster bed?
He:
Well, did you evah!
What a swell party this is!
She:
Lilly Lane has lousy luck,
She was there when the light'ning struck.
He:
Well, did you evah!
What a swell party this is!
It's fun, it's fine.
It's too divine.

(continues)

("Well, Did You Evah?" *continued*)

It's smooth, it's smart.
It's Rodgers, it's Hart!
What debs, what stags.
What gossip, what gags!
What feathers, what fuss!
She:
Just between the two of us,
Reggie's rather scatterbrained,
He dove in when the pool was drained.
He:
Well, did you evah!
What a swell party this is!
She:
Mrs. Smith in her new Hup
Crossed the bridge when the bridge was up.
He:
Well, did you evah!
What a swell party this is!

Refrain 4
He:
Have you heard that Mrs. Cass
Had three beers and then ate the glass?
She:
Well, did you evah!
What a swell party this is!
He:
Have you heard that Captain Craig
Breeds termites in his wooden leg?

She:
Well, did you evah!
What a swell party this is!
It's fun, it's fresh,
It's post depresh.
It's Shangrilah.
It's Harper's Bazaar!
What clothes, quel chic,
What pearls, they're the peak!
What glamour, what cheer!
He:
This will simply slay you, dear,
Kitty isn't paying calls,
She slipped over Niagara Falls.
She:
Well, did you evah!
What a swell party this is!
He:
Have you heard that Mayor Hague
Just came down with bubonic plague?
She:
Well, did you evah!
What a swell party this is!

What Did I Have That I Don't Have?

Words by Alan Jay Lerner
Music by Burton Lane

from *On a Clear Day You Can See Forever*

I don't see why they redesigned me,
He likes the way he used to find me.
He likes the girl I left behind me.
I mean, he…
I mean, me…

What did I have that I don't have?
What did he like that I lost track of?
What did I do, that I don't do
The way I did before?

What isn't there that once was there?
What have I got a great big lack of?
Something in me then
He could see then
Beckons to him no more.

I'm just a victim of time,
Obsolete in my prime!
Out of date and outclassed
By my past.

What did he love that there's none of?
What did I lose the sweet warm knack of?
Wouldn't I be the late, great me,
If I knew how? Oh!
What did I have I don't have now?

Where can I go to repair
All the wear and the tear?
Till I'm once again the—
Previous me?

What did he like that I'm not like?
What was the charm that I've run dry of?
What would I give if my old know-how
Still knew how! Oh!
What did I have I don't have now?

What Makes Me Love Him?

Words and Music by Jerry Bock and Sheldon Harnick

from *The Apple Tree*

What makes me love him?
It's not his singing.
I've heard his singing,
It sours the milk.
And yet,
It's gotten to the point
Where I prefer that kind of milk.

What makes me love him?
It's not his learning.
He's learned so slowly,
His whole life long.
And tho'
He really knows a multitude of things,
They're mostly wrong.

He is a good man,
Yet, I would love him
If he abused me,
Or used me ill.
And tho' he's handsome,
I know inside me,
Were he a plain man,
I'd love him still.

What makes me love him?
It's quite beyond me.
It must be something
I can't define,
Unless,
It's merely that he's masculine,
And that he's mine.

Where Is Love?

Words and Music by Lionel Bart

from the Broadway Musical *Oliver!*

Where is love?
Does it fall from skies above?
Is it underneath the willow tree
That I've been dreaming of?

Where is she
Who I close my eyes to see?
Will I ever know the sweet "hello"
That's meant for only me?

Who can say where she may hide?
Must I travel far and wide
Till I am beside the someone who
I can mean something to?
Where, where is love?

Every night I kneel and pray,
Let tomorrow be the day
When I see the face of someone who
I can mean something to?
Where, where is love?

Where Is the Life That Late I Led?

Words and Music by Cole Porter

from *Kiss Me, Kate*

Since I reached the charming age of puberty,
I began to finger feminine curls.
Like a show that's typically Shuberty,
I have always had a multitude of girls.
But now that a married man, at last, am I,
How aware of my dear, departed past am I.

Refrain:
Where is the life that late I led?
Where is it now?
Totally dead.
Where is the fun I used to find?
Where has it gone?
Gone with the wind.

A married life may all be well,
But raising an heir
Could never compare
With raising a bit of hell.
So I repeat what first I said,
Where is the life that late I—

In dear Milano,
Where are you, Momo?
Still selling those pictures of the scriptures
In the Duomo?
And Carolina,
Where are you Lina?
Still peddling your pizza in the streets o'
Taormina?

And in Firenze,
Where are you Alice?
Still there in your pretty, itty-bitty
Pitti palace?
And sweet Lucretia,
So young and gay-ee?
What scandalous doin's in the ruins
Of Pompeii!

Refrain

The marriage game is quite alright.
Yes, during the day,
It's easy to play,
But oh, what a bore at night.
So I repeat what first I said:
Where is the life that late I—

Where is Rebecca,
My Beck-i-weck-io?
Could still she be cruising that amusing
Ponte Vecchio?
Where is Fedora,
The wild virago?
It's lucky I missed her gangster sister
From Chicago.

Where is Venetia,
Who loved to chat so?
Could still she be drinkin' in her stinkin'
Pink palazzo?
And lovely Lisa,
Where are you Lisa?
You gave a new meaning to the leaning
Tow'r of Piza!

Refrain

I've oft' been told of nuptial bliss,
But what do you do,
At quarter to two,
With only a shrew to kiss?
So I repeat what first I said:
Where is the life that late I led?

Where or When

Words by Lorenz Hart
Music by Richard Rodgers

from *Babes in Arms*

When you're awake, the things you think
Come from the dreams you dream.
Thought has wings, and lots of things
Are seldom what they seem.
Sometimes you think you've lived before
All that you live today.
Things you do come back to you,
As though they knew the way.
Oh, the tricks the mind can play!

It seems we stood and talked like this before,
We looked at each other in the same way then,
But I can't remember where or when.
The clothes you're wearing are the clothes you wore,
The smile you are smiling you were smiling then.
But I can't remember where or when.
Some things that happen, for the first time
Seem to be happening again.
And so it seems that we have met before,
And laughed before, and loved before.
But who knows where or when!

Who Can I Turn To (When Nobody Needs Me)

Words and Music by Leslie Bricusse and Anthony Newley

from *The Roar of the Greasepaint—The Smell of the Crowd*

Who can I turn to
When nobody needs me?
My heart wants to know
And so I must go
Where destiny leads me.
With no star to guide me,
And no one beside me,
I'll go on my way,
And after the day,
The darkness will hide me.

And maybe tomorrow
I'll find what I'm after
I'll throw off my sorrow,
Beg, steal or borrow
My share of laughter,
With you I could learn to,
With you on a new day,
But who can I turn to
If you turn away?

Who Will Buy?

Words and Music by Lionel Bart

from the Broadway Musical *Oliver!*

Refrain 1:
Who will buy this wonderful morning?
Such a sky you never did see.
Who will tie it up with a ribbon,
And put it in a box for me?

So I can see it at my leisure,
Whenever things go wrong,
And I would keep it as a treasure
To last my whole life long.

Refrain 2:
Who will buy this wonderful feeling?
I'm so high, I swear I could fly.
Me, oh my, I don't want to lose it,
So what am I to do
To keep the sky so blue?
There must be someone who will buy.

Refrain 1

There'll never be a day so sunny,
It could not happen twice.
Where is the man with all the money?
It's cheap at half the price!

Refrain 2

ADDITIONAL LYRICS

Who will buy this morning of mornings?
Makes you feel you're walking on air.
Ev'ry tree and flower is singing,
"How fortunate are we
To be alive to see,
The dawning of a day so fair!"

Who will buy this wonderful feeling?
I'm so high, I swear I could fly.
What a sky! A heavenly ceiling,
Inviting you to come and buy!

Why Can't You Behave?

Words and Music by Cole Porter

from *Kiss Me, Kate*

Why can't you behave?
Oh, why can't you behave?
After all the things you told me
And the promises that you gave,
Oh, why can't you behave?

Why can't you be good?
And do just as you should?
Won't you turn that new leaf over,
So your baby can be your slave?
Oh, why can't you behave?

There's a farm I know
Near my old home town,
Where we two can go
And try settlin' down.

There I'll care for you forever,
'Cause you're all in the world I crave,
But why can't you behave?
(Gee, but I need you, kid!)
I always knew you did.
But why can't you behave?

Why Did I Choose You?

Lyric by Herbert Martin
Music by Michael Leonard

from *The Yearling*

Why did I choose you?
What did I see in you?
I saw the heart you hide so well;
I saw a quiet man who had a gentle way,
A way that caught me in its glowing spell.

Why did I want you?
What could you offer me?
A love to last a lifetime through.
And when I lost my heart so many years ago,
I lost it lovingly and willingly to you.
If I had to choose again, I would still choose you.

Wish You Were Here

Words and Music by Harold Rome

from *Wish You Were Here*

Where is it gone?

Refrain 1:
They're not making the skies
    as blue this year.
Wish you were here!
As blue as they used to when you were near.
Wish you were here!
And the mornings don't seem as new,
Brand new as they did with you.
Wish you were here!
Wish you were here!
Wish you were here!

Refrain 2:
Someone's painting the leaves all
    wrong this year.
Wish you were here!
And why did the birds change
    their song this year?
Wish you were here!
They're not shining the stars as bright.
They've stolen the joy from the night!
Wish you were here!
Wish you were here!
Wish you were here!

Where is the wonder
As each day would start,
That sang with the dawn,
Ran away with my heart?
Where is it gone?

Refrain 1

Refrain 2

Why Do the Wrong People Travel?

Words and Music by Noel Coward

from *Sail Away*

Travel, they say, improves the mind,
An irritating platitude,
Which frankly, *entre-nous*,
Is very far from true.

Personally, I've yet to find
That longitude and latitude
Can educate those scores
Of monumental bores,

Who travel in groups and herds and troupes
Of various breeds and sexes,
Till the whole world reels to shouts and
    squeals
And the clicking of Roliflexes.

Why do the wrong people travel,
    travel, travel,
When the right people stay back home?
What compulsion compels them
And who the hell tells them
To drag their bags to Zanzibar
Instead of staying quietly in Omaha?

The Taj Mahal and the Grand Canal
And the sunny French Riviera
Would be less oppressed if the Middle West
Would settle for somewhere rather nearer.

Please do not think that I criticize or cavil
At a genuine urge to roam.
But why, oh why, do the wrong people travel
When the right people stay back home,
And mind their bus'ness,
When the right people stay back home,
With television,
When the right people stay back home,
I'm merely asking,
Why the right people stay back home?

Just when you think romance is ripe,
It rather sharply dawns on you
That each sweet serenade
Is for the tourist trade.

Any attractive native type
Who resolutely fawns on you
Will give as his address
American Express.

There isn't a rock between Bangkok
And beaches of Hispianola
That does not recoil from suntan oil
And the gurgle of Coca Cola.

Why do the wrong people travel,
    travel, travel,
When the right people stay back home?
What explains this mass mania
To leave Pennsylvania,
And clack around like flocks of geese,
Demanding dry martinis on the Isles of Greece?

In the smallest street, where the
    gourmets meet,
They invariably fetch up,
And it's hard to make them accept a steak
That isn't served rare and served
    with ketchup.

It would take years to unravel, ravel, ravel
Ev'ry impulse that makes them roam.
But why, oh why, do the wrong people travel
When the right people stay back home,
And eat hot doughnuts,
When the right people stay back home,
With all that lettuce,
When the right people stay back home,
I sometimes wonder
Why the right people stay back home?

Why do the wrong people travel,
    travel, travel,
When the right people stay back home?
What peculiar obsessions
Inspire those processions
Of families from Houston, Tex.,
With all those cameras around their necks?

They will take a train or an aeroplane
For an hour on the Costa Brava,
And they'll see Pompeii on the only day
That it's up to its ears in molten lava.

Millions of tourists are churning
    up the gravel,
While they gaze at St. Peter's Dome.
But why, oh why, do the wrong people travel
When the right people stay back home,
And play canasta,
When the right people stay back home,
Won't someone tell me,
Why the right people stay back home?

Wishing You Were Somehow Here Again

Music by Andrew Lloyd Webber
Lyrics by Charles Hart
Additional Lyrics by Richard Stilgoe

from *The Phantom of the Opera*

You were once my one companion,
You were all that mattered.
You were once a friend and father,
Then my world was shattered.

Wishing you were somehow here again,
Wishing you were somehow near,
Sometimes it seemed
If I just dreamed,
Somehow you would be here.

Wishing I could hear your voice again,
Knowing that I never would,
Dreaming of you
Won't help me to do
All that you dreamed I could.

Passing bells and sculpted angels,
Cold and monumental,
Seem for you the wrong companions,
You were warm and gentle.

Too many years,
Fighting back tears,
Why can't the past just die?

Wishing you were somehow here again,
Knowing we must say good-bye.
Try to forgive,
Teach me to live,
Give me the strength to try.

No more memories, no more silent tears,
No more gazing across the wasted years.
Help me say good-bye!
Help me say good-bye!

With a Little Bit of Luck

Words by Alan Jay Lerner
Music by Frederick Loewe

from *My Fair Lady*

The Lord above gave man an arm of iron,
So he could do his job and never shirk.
The Lord above gave man an arm
    of iron, but
With a little bit of luck, with a little
    bit of luck,
Someone else'll do the blinkin' work!
With a little bit, with a little bit,
With a little bit of luck, you'll never work!

The Lord above made liquor for temptation,
To see if man could turn away from sin.
The Lord above made liquor for
    temptation, but
With a little bit of luck, with a little
    bit of luck,
When temptation comes, you'll give right in!
With a little bit, with a little bit,
With a little bit of luck, you'll give right in!

Oh, you can walk the straight and narrow,
But with a little bit of luck you'll run amuck!

The gentle sex was made for man to marry,
To share his nest and see his food is cooked.
The gentle sex was made for man
    to marry, but
With a little bit of luck, with a little
    bit of luck,
You can have it all and not get hooked.
With a little bit, with a little bit,
With a little bit of luck, you won't
    get hooked!

Refrain:
With a little bit, with a little bit,
With a little bit of bloomin' luck!

The Lord above made man to help
    his neighbor,
No matter where, on land, or sea, or foam.
The Lord above made man to help his
    neighbor, but
(Whispered:)
With a little bit of luck, with a little
    bit of luck,
(Sung:)
When he comes around you won't be home!
With a little bit, with a little bit,
With a little bit of luck, you won't be home!

They're always throwin' goodness at you,
But with a little bit of luck, a man can duck!

Oh, it's a crime for man to go philandrin',
And fill his wife's poor heart with
    grief and doubt.
Oh, it's a crime for man to go
    philandrin', but
With a little bit of luck, with a little
    bit of luck,
You can see the bloodhound don't find out!
With a little bit, with a little bit,
With a little bit of luck, she won't find out!

Refrain

With a Song in My Heart

Words by Lorenz Hart
Music by Richard Rodgers

from *Spring Is Here*

Though I know that we meet every night
And we couldn't have changed since
  the last time,
To my joy and delight,
It's a new kind of love at first sight.
Though it's you and it's I all the time,
Every meeting's a marvelous pastime.
You're increasingly sweet,
So whenever we happen to meet
I greet you…

Refrain:
With a song in my heart
I behold your adorable face.
Just a song at the start,
But it soon is a hymn to your grace.
When the music swells
I'm touching your hand;
It tells that you're standing near, and…
At the sound of your voice
Heaven opens its portals to me.
Can I help but rejoice
That a song such as ours came to be?
But I always knew
I would live life through,
With a song in my heart for you.

Oh, the moon's not a moon for a night
And these stars will not twinkle and fade out,
And the words in my ears
Will resound for the rest of my years.
In the morning I'll find with delight
Not a note of music is played out.
It will be just as sweet,
And an air that I'll live to repeat,
I greet you…

Refrain

Wouldn't It Be Loverly

Words by Alan Jay Lerner
Music by Frederick Loewe

from *My Fair Lady*

All I want is a room somewhere,
Far away from the cold night air,
With one enormous chair,
Oh, wouldn't it be loverly?

Lots of choc'late for me to eat,
Lots of coal makin' lots of heat,
Warm face, warm hands, warm feet,
Oh, wouldn't it be loverly?

Oh, so loverly sittin'
Abso-bloomin'-lutely still!
I would never budge 'til
Spring crept over me windersill.

Someone's head restin' on my knee,
Warm and tender as he can be,
Who takes good care of me,
Oh, wouldn't it be loverly?
Loverly!

Written in the Stars

Music by Elton John
Lyrics by Tim Rice

from Walt Disney Theatrical Production *Aida*

Male:
I am here to tell you we can never
  meet again.
Simple really, isn't it?
A word or two and then a lifetime of
  not knowing
Where or why or when.
You think of me or speak of me
Or wonder what befell
The someone you once loved
So long ago so well.

Female:
Never wonder what I'll feel as
  living shuffles by.
You don't have to ask me and
  I need not reply.
Every moment of my life from now until I die
I will think or dream of you and fail to
  understand
How a perfect love can be confounded
  out of hand.

Both:
Is it written in the stars?
Are we paying for some crime?
Is that all that we are good for,
Just a stretch of mortal time?
Is this God's experiment in which
  we have no say?
In which we're given paradise,
  but only for a day.

Male:
Nothing can be altered.
  Oh, there is nothing to decide.
No escape, no change of heart nor
  any place to hide.

Female:
You are all I'll ever want but this
  I am denied.
Sometimes in my darkest thoughts
I wish I never learned what it is
To be in love and have that love returned.

Both:
Is it written in the stars?
Are we paying for some crime?
Is that all that we are good for,
Just a stretch of mortal time?
Is this God's experiment in which
  we have no say?
In which we're given paradise,
  but only for a day.
Is it written in the stars?
Are we paying for some crime?
Is that all that we are good for,
Just a stretch of mortal time?

Male:
In which we have no say?

Female:
In which we're given paradise only

Both:
For a day.

Wunderbar

Words and Music by Cole Porter

from *Kiss Me, Kate*

Refrain:
Wunderbar,
Wunderbar!
There's our fav'rite star above.
What a bright, shining star!
Like our love, it's wunderbar!

Gazing down on the Jungfrau,
From our secret chalet for two,
Let us drink, Liebchen mein,
In the moonlight benign,
To the joy of our dream come true.

Wunderbar,
Wunderbar!
What a perfect night for love,
Here I am, here you are,
Why, it's truly wunderbar!

Wunderbar,
Wunderbar!
We're alone and hand in glove,
Not a cloud near or far,
Why, it's more than wunderbar!

Say you care, dear.
(For you madly.)
Say you long, dear.
(For your kiss.)
Do you swear, dear?
(Darling, gladly.)
Life's divine, dear,
(And you're mine, dear!)

Refrain

And you're mine, dear!

Refrain

You Are Beautiful

Lyrics by Oscar Hammerstein II
Music by Richard Rodgers

from *Flower Drum Song*

You are beautiful,
Small and shy,
You are the girl whose eyes met mine
Just as your boat sailed by.

This I know of you,
Nothing more:
You are the girl whose eyes met mine,
Passing the river shore.

You are the girl whose laugh I heard,
Silver and soft and bright;
Soft as the fall of lotus leaves
Brushing the air of night.

While your flower boat
Sailed away,
Gently your eyes looked back on mine,
Clearly you heard me say:
"You are the girl I will love someday."

You Musn't Kick It Around

Words by Lorenz Hart
Music by Richard Rodgers

from *Pal Joey*

If my heart gets in your hair,
You musn't kick it around,
If you're bored with this affair,
You musn't kick it around.

Even though I'm mild and meek,
When we have a brawl.
If I turn the other cheek,
You musn't kick it at all.

When I try to ring the bell,
You never care for the sound,
The next guy may not do as well,
You musn't kick it around.

You Walk with Me

Words and Music by David Yazbek

from *The Full Monty*

Is it the wind
Over my shoulder?
Is it the wind
That I hear gently whispering,

"Are you alone,
There in the valley?"
No, not alone, for you walk,
You walk with me.

Refrain:
Is it the wind there,
Over my shoulder?
Is it your voice calling quietly?
Over the hilltop,
Down in the valley,
Never alone, for you walk with me.

When evening falls,
And the air gets colder,
When shadows cover the road
I am following.

Will I be alone,
There in the darkness?
No, not alone,
Not alone, and I'll never be.
Never alone.
You are walking,
You're walking with me.

Refrain

Over the hilltop,
Down in the valley,
Never alone, for you walk with me.
Never alone, for you walk with me.

You'll Never Get Away from Me

Words by Stephen Sondheim
Music by Jule Styne

from *Gypsy*

Refrain
Rose:
You'll never get away from me.
You can climb the tallest tree,
I'll be there somehow.
True, you could say, "Hey, here's your hat,"
But a little thing like that
Couldn't stop me now.

I couldn't get away from you,
Even if you told me to,
So go on and try!
Just try,
And you're gonna see,
How you're gonna not at all
Get away from me.

Herbie:
Rose, I love you,
But don't count your chickens.
Rose:
Come dance with me.
Herbie:
I warn you that I'm no boy scout.
Rose:
Relax a while.
Come dance with me.
Herbie:
So don't think
That I'm easy pickin's.
Rose:
The music's so nice.

Herbie:
Rose!
'Cause I just may some day
Pick up and pack out.
Rose:
Oh, no you won't,
No, not a chance.
No arguments,
Shut up and dance.

Rose:
Refrain

Both:
I couldn't get away from you,
Even if I wanted to,
Rose:
Well, go on and try!
Just try,
Herbie:
Ah, Rose!
Rose:
And you're gonna see,
Herbie:
Ah, Rose!
Rose:
How you're gonna not at all
Get away from me.

You're a Builder Upper

Lyric by Ira Gershwin and E.Y. Harburg
Music by Harold Arlen

from *Life Begins at 8:40*

When you want to,
You are able
To make me feel
That I'm Clark Gable,
Then, next minute,
You make me feel
I'm something from the zoo.

First you warm up,
Then you're distant,
Never knew a girl
So inconsistent.
I'm a big shot
At half past one,
A so-and-so by two.

Heaven forgive you for your sins,
Keeping me on needles and pins!

Refrain:
You're a builder upper,
A breaker downer,
A holder outer,
And I'm a giver in-er.

Sad, but true,
I'm a sap-a-roo, too,
Taking it from
A taker-over like you.

Don't know where I'm ata,
I'm just a this-a,
Then I'm a that-a,
A taker on the chin-er.

My, my, my,
What a weaky am I,
To love you
As I do.

Just when I'm ready to sob,
You hand me a throb,
And ev'rything is hunky dory,
And that's my story.
Open your arms,
And I'm a stooge for your charms.

Refrain

Sad, but true,
I love it, I do!
Being broken by
A builder upper like you.

You're Never Fully Dressed Without a Smile

Lyric by Martin Charnin
Music by Charles Strouse

from *Annie*

O—X—Y—D—E—N—T!

Hey, hobo man,
Hey, Dapper Dan,
You've both got your style,
But brother,
You're never fully dressed without a smile.

Your clothes may be
Beau Brummelly,
They stand out a mile,
But brother,
You're never fully dressed without a smile.

Who cares what they're wearing
On Main Street or Saville Row?
It's what you wear from ear to ear
And not from head to toe that matters.

So, Senator,
So, janitor,
So long for a while,
Remember,
You're never fully dressed without a—

Doo doodle-oo...

Your clothes may be
Beau Brummelly,
They stand out a mile,
But brother,
You're never fully dressed,
You're never dressed without a
S—M—I—L—E.
Smile, darn ya.

You're the Cream in My Coffee

Words and Music by B.G. DeSylva, Lew Brown and Ray Henderson

from *Hold Everything*

You're the cream in my coffee,
You're the salt in my stew.
You will always be
My necessity,
I'd be lost without you.

You're the starch in my collar,
You're the lace in my shoe.
You will always be
My necessity,
I'd be lost without you.

Most men tell love-tales,
And each phrase dovetails,
You've heard each known way,
This way is my own way.

Refrain:
You're the sail of my love-boat,
You're the captain and crew.
You will always be
My necessity,
I'd be lost without you.

You give life savor,
Bring out its flavor,
So this is clear, dear,
You're my Worcestershire, dear.

Refrain

You've Got to Be Carefully Taught

Lyrics by Oscar Hammerstein II
Music by Richard Rodgers

from *South Pacific*

You've got to be carefully taught to hate and fear.
You've got to be taught from year to year.
It's got to be drummed in your dear little ear.
You've got to be carefully taught.

You've got to be taught to be afraid
Of people whose eyes are oddly made,
And people whose skin is a different shade,
You've got to be carefully taught.

You've got to be taught before it's too late,
Before you are six, or seven, or eight,
To hate all the people your relatives hate,
You've got to be carefully taught!
You've got to be carefully taught!

Young and Foolish

Words by Arnold B. Horwitt
Music by Albert Hague

from *Plain and Fancy*

Once we were foolish children,
Playing as children play.
Racing thro' a meadow, April bright,
Dreaming on a hilltop half the night.

Now that we're growing older,
We have no time to play.
Now that we're growing wiser,
We are not wise enough to stay—

Young and foolish,
Why is it wrong to be
Young and foolish,
We haven't long to be.
Soon enough, the carefree days,
The sunlit days go by.
Soon enough the bluebird
Has to fly.

We were foolish,
One day we fell in love,
Now, we wonder
What we were dreaming of.

Refrain:
Smiling in the sunlight,
Laughing in the rain,
I wish that we were
Young and foolish again.

Refrain

Younger Than Springtime

Lyrics by Oscar Hammerstein II
Music by Richard Rodgers

from *South Pacific*

I touch your hand,
And my arms grow strong,
Like a pair of birds
That burst with song.
My eyes look down
At your lovely face,
And I hold the world
In my embrace.

Younger than springtime are you,
Softer than starlight are you,
Warmer than winds of June
Are the gentle lips you gave me.
Gayer than laughter are you,
Sweeter than music are you.
Angel and lover, heaven and earth,
Are you to me.
And when your youth and joy invade my arms
And fill my heart, as now they do,
Then, younger than springtime am I,
Gayer than laughter am I,
Angel and lover, heaven and earth,
Am I with you.

Your Feet's Too Big

Words and Music by Fred Fisher and Ada Benson

from *Ain't Misbehavin'*

Say in indoor sports,
It's there where you shine,
In washin' the dishes baby,
You're divine.
You shine when it comes to sports
For swimmin' and duckin',
Oh, Boy!
When it comes to truckin',

Refrain:
Your feet's too big,
Don't want you, 'cause
Your feet's too big,
Mad at you, 'cause
Your feet's too big,
Hates you, 'cause
Your feet's too big.
Shwa-shwa-bo…

Your girl she likes you,
And thinks you are nice,
You got what it takes
To be in paradise,
She said that she likes your face
And she likes your rig,
Oh, man!
But your feet's too big.

Refrain

Up in Harlem, at
A table for two,
There were four of us,
Me, your big feet and you.
From your ankle up, I'll say
That you sure are sweet,
From there down,
You're too much feet.

Refrain

When you go and die,
Nobody will sob,
That old undertaker
Will have quite a job.
You'll look mighty funny
When you lay in that casket,
Your feet,
Stickin' out that basket!

Refrain

She said the first time,
We met on the street,
And strange as it seems,
She didn't see my feet,
We saw two holdup men,
And we thought they would scare us,
They yelled,
"Look at those Carneros!"

Refrain

Show Index

Songwriter Index

Bob Merrill
137 The Music That Makes Me Dance
156 People

Irving Mills
34 Caravan
131 Mood Indigo
173 Solitude

Jean-Marc Natel
42 Do You Hear the People Sing?
151 On My Own

Anthony Newley
55 Gonna Build a Mountain
154 Once in a Lifetime
213 Who Can I Turn To
       (When Nobody Needs Me)

Trevor Nunn
128 Memory
151 On My Own

Cole Porter
8 Ace in the Hole
12 All I've Got to Get Now
       Is My Man
13 All of You
15 Another Op'nin', Another Show
43 Down in the Depths
       (On the Ninetieth Floor)
46 Ev'ry Time We Say Goodbye
50 Friendship
72 I Hate You, Darling
75 I Love Paris
76 I Love You
98 It's De-Lovely
110 Let's Not Talk About Love
113 A Little Rumba Numba
116 A Little Skipper from
       Heaven Above
138 My Heart Belongs to Daddy
170 Siberia
172 So in Love
204 Well, Did You Evah?
210 Where Is the Life That Late I Led?
215 Why Can't You Behave?
225 Wunderbar

Amy Powers
17 As If We Never Said Goodbye

Andy Razaf
9 Ain't Misbehavin'

Emelia Renaud
175 Somebody Loves Me

Herbert Reynolds
189 They Didn't Believe Me

Tim Rice
36 Close Every Door
224 Written in the Stars

Jay Rifkin
192 They Live in You

Mary Rodgers
124 Many Moons Ago

Richard Rodgers
40 Dancing on the Ceiling
41 Do-Re-Mi
44 Edelweiss
47 A Fellow Needs a Girl
52 The Gentleman Is a Dope
53 Getting to Know You
54 Glad to Be Unhappy
59 Have You Met Miss Jones?
60 He Was Too Good to Me
69 I Could Write a Book
73 I Have Dreamed
92 If I Loved You
95 It Might as Well Be Spring
96 It Never Entered My Mind
101 June Is Bustin' Out All Over
106 The Lady Is a Tramp
120 Love, Look Away
129 Mister Snow
134 The Most Beautiful Girl
       in the World
139 My Heart Stood Still
141 My Romance
155 Out of My Dreams
157 People Will Say We're in Love
166 Sentimental Me
174 Some Enchanted Evening
180 The Sound of Music
186 The Surrey with the
       Fringe on Top
188 There's a Small Hotel
194 Thou Swell
201 Wait Till You See Her
202 We Kiss in a Shadow
212 Where or When
222 With a Song in My Heart
226 You Are Beautiful
227 You Mustn't Kick It Around
233 You've Got to Be Carefully Taught
235 Younger Than Springtime

Sigmund Romberg
35 Close as Pages in a Book
121 Lover, Come Back to Me

Harold Rome
18 Be Kind to Your Parents
146 Nobody Makes a Pass at Me
217 Wish You Were Here

Arthur Rose
126 Me and My Girl

Billy Rose
70 I Found a Million Dollar Baby
       (In a Five and Ten Cent Store)

William Rose
133 More Than You Know

Carole Bayer Sager
79 I Still Believe in Love

Milton Schafer
168 She (He) Touched Me

Harvey Schmidt
74 I Love My Wife
135 Much More
178 Soon It's Gonna Rain

Claude-Michel Schönberg
24 Bring Him Home
42 Do You Hear the People Sing?
45 Empty Chairs at Empty Tables
81 I'd Give My Life for You
103 The Last Night of the World
151 On My Own
181 Stars
183 Sun and Moon

Stephen Schwartz
10 All Good Gifts
153 On the Willows

Stephen Sondheim
11 All I Need Is the Girl
16 Anyone Can Whistle
28 Buddy's Blues
38 Could I Leave You
48 Everybody Ought to Have a Maid
88 I'm Still Here
94 In Buddy's Eyes
104 The Ladies Who Lunch
171 Small World
177 Sorry-Grateful
185 That'll Show Him
198 Together Wherever We Go
229 You'll Never Get Away from Me

Richard Stilgoe
136 The Music of the Night
220 Wishing You Were Somehow
       Here Again

Billy Strayhorn
159 Satin Doll

Charles Strouse
143 N.Y.C.
231 You're Never Fully Dressed
       Without a Smile

Jule Styne
11 All I Need Is the Girl
102 Just in Time
137 The Music That Makes Me Dance
144 Never Never Land
156 People
171 Small World
198 Together Wherever We Go
229 You'll Never Get Away from Me

Juan Tizol
34 Caravan

More Collections from The Lyric Library

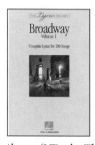

BROADWAY VOLUME I

An invaluable collection of lyrics to 200 top Broadway tunes, including: All at Once You Love Her • All I Ask of You • And All That Jazz • Any Dream Will Do • As Long As He Needs Me • At the End of the Day • Autumn in New York • Bali Ha'i • Bewitched • Cabaret • Castle on a Cloud • Climb Ev'ry Mountain • Comedy Tonight • Don't Rain on My Parade • Everything's Coming up Roses • Hello, Dolly! • I Could Have Danced All Night • I Dreamed a Dream • I Remember It Well • If I Were a Bell • It's the Hard-Knock Life • Let Me Entertain You • Mame • My Funny Valentine • Oklahoma • Seasons of Love • September Song • Seventy Six Trombones • Shall We Dance? • Springtime for Hitler • Summer Nights • Tomorrow • Try to Remember • Unexpected Song • What I Did for Love • With One Look • You'll Never Walk Alone • (I Wonder Why?) You're Just in Love • and more.

_____00240201 ....$14.95

BROADWAY VOLUME II

200 more favorite Broadway lyrics (with no duplication from Volume I): Ain't Misbehavin' • All of You • Another Op'nin', Another Show • As If We Never Said Goodbye • Beauty School Dropout • The Best of Times • Bring Him Home • Brotherhood of Man • Camelot • Close Every Door • Consider Yourself • Do-Re-Mi • Edelweiss • Getting to Know You • Have You Met Miss Jones? • I Loved You Once in Silence • I'm Flying • If Ever I Would Leave You • The Impossible Dream (The Quest) • It Only Takes a Moment • The Lady Is a Tramp • The Last Night of the World • A Little More Mascara • Lost in the Stars • Love Changes Everything • Me and My Girl • Memory • My Heart Belongs to Daddy • On a Clear Day (You Can See Forever) • On My Own • People • Satin Doll • The Sound of Music • Sun and Moon • The Surrey with the Fringe on Top • Unusual Way (In a Very Unusual Way) • We Kiss in a Shadow • We Need a Little Christmas • Who Will Buy? • Wishing You Were Somehow Here Again • Younger Than Springtime • and more.

_____00240205 ....$14.95

CHRISTMAS

200 lyrics to the most loved Christmas songs of all time, including: Angels We Have Heard on High • Auld Lang Syne • Away in a Manger • Baby, It's Cold Outside • The Chipmunk Song • The Christmas Shoes • The Christmas Song (Chestnuts Roasting on an Open Fire) • Christmas Time Is Here • Do They Know It's Christmas? • Do You Hear What I Hear • Feliz Navidad • The First Noel • Frosty the Snow Man • The Gift • God Rest Ye Merry, Gentlemen • Goin' on a Sleighride • Grandma Got Run over by a Reindeer • Happy Xmas (War Is Over) • He Is Born, the Holy Child (Il Est Ne, Le Divin Enfant) • The Holly and the Ivy • A Holly Jolly Christmas • (There's No Place Like) Home for the Holidays • I Heard the Bells on Christmas Day • I Wonder As I Wander • I'll Be Home for Christmas • I've Got My Love to Keep Me Warm • In the Bleak Midwinter • It Came upon the Midnight Clear • It's Beginning to Look like Christmas • It's Just Another New Year's Eve • Jingle Bells • Joy to the World • Mary, Did You Know? • Merry Christmas, Darling • The Most Wonderful Time of the Year • My Favorite Things • Rudolph the Red-Nosed Reindeer • Silent Night • Silver Bells • The Twelve Days of Christmas • What Child Is This? • What Made the Baby Cry? • Wonderful Christmastime • and more.

_____00240206 ....$14.95

See our website for a complete contents list for each volume:
www.halleonard.com

FOR MORE INFORMATION, SEE YOUR LOCAL MUSIC DEALER,
OR WRITE TO:

HAL•LEONARD®
CORPORATION
7777 W. BLUEMOUND RD. P.O. BOX 13819 MILWAUKEE, WI 53213

Prices, contents and availability subject to change without notice.

More Collections from The Lyric Library

CLASSIC ROCK

Lyrics to 200 essential rock classics songs, including: All Day and All of the Night • All Right Now • Angie • Another One Bites the Dust • Back in the U.S.S.R. • Ballroom Blitz • Barracuda • Beast of Burden • Bell Bottom Blues • Brain Damage • Brass in Pocket • Breakdown • Breathe • Bus Stop • California Girls • Carry on Wayward Son • Centerfold • Changes • Cocaine • Cold As Ice • Come Sail Away • Come Together • Crazy Little Thing Called Love • Crazy on You • Don't Do Me like That • Don't Fear the Reaper • Don't Let the Sun Go down on Me • Don't Stand So Close to Me • Dreamer • Drive My Car • Dust in the Wind • 867-5309/Jenny • Emotional Rescue • Every Breath You Take • Every Little Thing She Does Is Magic • Eye in the Sky • Eye of the Tiger • Fame • Forever Young • Fortress Around Your Heart • Free Ride • Give a Little Bit • Gloria • Godzilla • Green-Eyed Lady • Heartache Tonight • Heroes • Hey Joe • Hot Blooded • I Fought the Law • I Shot the Sheriff • I Won't Back Down • Instant Karma • Invisible Touch • It's Only Rock 'N' Roll (But I like It) • It's Still Rock and Roll to Me • Layla • The Logical Song • Long Cool Woman (In a Black Dress) • Love Hurts • Maggie May • Me and Bobby McGee • Message in a Bottle • Mississippi Queen • Money • Money for Nothing • My Generation • New Kid in Town • Nights in White Satin • Paradise by the Dashboard Light • Piano Man • Rebel, Rebel • Refugee • Rhiannon • Roxanne • Shattered • Smoke on the Water • Sultans of Swing • Sweet Emotion • Walk This Way • We Gotta Get Out of This Place • We Will Rock You • Wouldn't It Be Nice • and many more!

_____00240183 ....$14.95

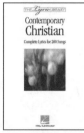

CONTEMPORARY CHRISTIAN

An amazing collection of 200 lyrics from some of the most prominent Contemporary Christian artists: Abba (Father) • After the Rain • Angels • Awesome God • Breathe on Me • Circle of Friends • Doubly Good to You • Down on My Knees • El Shaddai • Father's Eyes • Friends • Give It Away • Go Light Your World • God's Own Fool • Grand Canyon • The Great Adventure • The Great Divide • He Walked a Mile • Heaven and Earth • Heaven in the Real World • His Strength Is Perfect • Household of Faith • How Beautiful • I Surrender All • Jesus Freak • Joy in the Journey • Judas' Kiss • A Little More • Live Out Loud • Love Will Be Our Home • A Maze of Grace • The Message • My Utmost for His Highest • Oh Lord, You're Beautiful • People Need the Lord • Pray • Say the Name • Signs of Life • Speechless • Stand • Steady On • Via Dolorosa • The Warrior Is a Child • What Matters Most • Would I Know You • and more.

_____00240184 ....$14.95

COUNTRY

A great resource of lyrics to 200 of the best country songs of all time, including: Act Naturally • All My Ex's Live in Texas • All the Gold in California • Always on My Mind • Amazed • American Made • Angel of the Morning • Big Bad John • Blue • Blue Eyes Crying in the Rain • Boot Scootin' Boogie • Breathe • By the Time I Get to Phoenix • Could I Have This Dance • Crazy • Daddy's Hands • D-I-V-O-R-C-E • Down at the Twist and Shout • Elvira • Folsom Prison Blues • Friends in Low Places • The Gambler • Grandpa (Tell Me 'Bout the Good Old Days) • Harper Valley P.T.A. • He Thinks He'll Keep Her • Hey, Good Lookin' • I Fall to Pieces • I Hope You Dance • I Love a Rainy Night • I Saw the Light • I've Got a Tiger by the Tail • Islands in the Stream • Jambalaya (On the Bayou) • The Keeper of the Stars • King of the Road • Lucille • Make the World Go Away • Mammas Don't Let Your Babies Grow up to Be Cowboys • My Baby Thinks He's a Train • Okie from Muskogee • Ring of Fire • Rocky Top • Sixteen Tons • Stand by Me • There's a Tear in My Beer • Walkin' After Midnight • When You Say Nothing at All • Where the Stars and Stripes and the Eagle Fly • Where Were You (When the World Stopped Turning) • You Are My Sunshine • Your Cheatin' Heart • and more.

_____00240204 ....$14.95

See our website for a complete contents list for each volume:
www.halleonard.com

FOR MORE INFORMATION, SEE YOUR LOCAL MUSIC DEALER,
OR WRITE TO:

HAL•LEONARD®
CORPORATION
7777 W. BLUEMOUND RD. P.O. BOX 13819 MILWAUKEE, WI 53213

Prices, contents and availability subject to change without notice.

More Collections from The Lyric Library

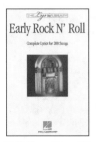

EARLY ROCK 'N' ROLL

Lyrics to 200 top songs that started the rock 'n' roll revolution, including: All I Have to Do Is Dream • All Shook Up • At the Hop • Baby Love • Barbara Ann • Be-Bop-A-Lula • Big Girls Don't Cry • Blue Suede Shoes • Bo Diddley • Book of Love • Calendar Girl • Chantilly Lace • Charlie Brown • Crying • Dancing in the Street • Do Wah Diddy Diddy • Don't Be Cruel (To a Heart That's True) • Earth Angel • Fun, Fun, Fun • Great Balls of Fire • He's a Rebel • Heatwave (Love Is like a Heatwave) • Hello Mary Lou • Hound Dog • I Walk the Line • It's My Party • Kansas City • The Loco-Motion • My Boyfriend's Back • My Guy • Oh, Pretty Woman • Peggy Sue • Rock and Roll Is Here to Stay • Sixteen Candles • Splish Splash • Stand by Me • Stupid Cupid • Surfin' U.S.A. • Teen Angel • A Teenager in Love • Twist and Shout • Walk like a Man • Where the Boys Are • Why Do Fools Fall in Love • Willie and the Hand Jive • and more.

_____00240203 ....$14.95

LOVE SONGS

Lyrics to 200 of the most romantic songs ever written, including: All My Loving • Always in My Heart (Siempre En Mi Corazon) • And I Love Her • Anniversary Song • Beautiful in My Eyes • Call Me Irresponsible • Can You Feel the Love Tonight • Cheek to Cheek • (They Long to Be) Close to You • Could I Have This Dance • Dedicated to the One I Love • Don't Know Much • Dream a Little Dream of Me • Endless Love • Fields of Gold • For Once in My Life • Grow Old with Me • The Hawaiian Wedding Song (Ke Kali Nei Au) • Heart and Soul • Hello, Young Lovers • How Deep Is the Ocean (How High Is the Sky) • I Just Called to Say I Love You • I'll Be There • I've Got My Love to Keep Me Warm • Just the Way You Are • Longer • L-O-V-E • Love Will Keep Us Together • Misty • Moonlight in Vermont • More (Ti Guardero' Nel Cuore) • My Funny Valentine • My Heart Will Go on (Love Theme from 'Titanic') • She • Speak Softly, Love (Love Theme) • Till • A Time for Us (Love Theme) • Unchained Melody • Up Where We Belong • We've Only Just Begun • What the World Needs Now Is Love • When I Fall in Love • Witchcraft • Wonderful Tonight • You Are the Sunshine of My Life • You're the Inspiration • You've Made Me So Very Happy • and more!

_____00240186 ....$14.95

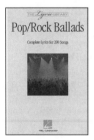

POP/ROCK BALLADS

Lyrics to 200 top tunes of the pop/rock era, including: Adia • After the Love Has Gone • Against All Odds (Take a Look at Me Now) • Always on My Mind • Amazed • And So It Goes • Baby What a Big Surprise • Ben • Breathe • Change the World • Come to My Window • Do You Know Where You're Going To? • Don't Cry Out Loud • Don't Fall in Love with a Dreamer • Don't Let Me Be Lonely Tonight • Easy • Feelings (¿Dime?) • Fire and Rain • From a Distance • Georgia on My Mind • Hero • I Hope You Dance • Imagine • In the Air Tonight • Iris • Just My Imagination (Running Away with Me) • Killing Me Softly with His Song • Laughter in the Rain • Looks like We Made It • My Heart Will Go on (Love Theme from 'Titanic') • New York State of Mind • The Rainbow Connection • Rainy Days and Mondays • Sailing • She's Always a Woman • Sing • Sunshine on My Shoulders • Take Me Home, Country Roads • Tears in Heaven • There You'll Be • Time After Time • Vision of Love • The Way We Were • Woman in Love • You're the Inspiration • You've Got a Friend • and more.

_____00240187 ....$14.95

See our website for a complete contents list for each volume:
www.halleonard.com

FOR MORE INFORMATION, SEE YOUR LOCAL MUSIC DEALER,
OR WRITE TO:

HAL•LEONARD®
CORPORATION
7777 W. BLUEMOUND RD. P.O. BOX 13819 MILWAUKEE, WI 53213

Prices, contents and availability subject to change without notice.